CAPITAN **CHIQUITO**

CAPITAN CHIQUITO

A Personal History of an Apache Chief,
1821–1919

JOHN PAUL HARTMAN

FOREWORD BY KARL JACOBY

TEXAS A&M UNIVERSITY PRESS

College Station

This paper meets the requirements of
ANSI/NISO Z39.48–1992 (Permanence of Paper).
Binding materials have been chosen for durability.

Manufactured in the United States of America

Library of Congress Cataloging-in-Publication Data

Names: Hartman, John Paul, 1951– author. | Jacoby, Karl, 1965– writer of foreword.
Title: Capitan Chiquito: a personal history of an Apache Chief, 1821–1919
/ John Paul Hartman; foreword by Karl Jacoby.
Other titles: Elma Dill Russell Spencer series in the West and Southwest; no. 47.
Description: First edition. | College Station: Texas A&M University Press,
[2022] | Series: Elma Dill Russell Spencer Series in the West and
Southwest; Number Forty-Seven | Includes bibliographical references and index.
Identifiers: LCCN 2021040671 (print) | LCCN 2021040672 (ebook) | ISBN
9781623499976 (cloth) | ISBN 9781623499983 (ebook)
Subjects: LCSH: Capitan Chiquito (Apache Chief), 1821–1919. | Apache
Indians—Kings and rulers—Biography. | Apache
Indians—Arizona—Aravaipa Canyon—History—19th century. | Camp Grant
Massacre, Ariz., 1871—Biography. | San Carlos Indian Reservation
(Ariz.)—Biography. | BISAC: BIOGRAPHY & AUTOBIOGRAPHY / Cultural,
Ethnic & Regional / Indigenous | HISTORY / United States / State & Local
/ Southwest (AZ, NM, OK, TX)
Classification: LCC E99.A6 H255 2022 (print) | LCC E99.A6 (ebook) | DDC
979.004/97250092 [B]—dc23

LC record available at https://lccn.loc.gov/2021040671
LC ebook record available at https://lccn.loc.gov/2021040672

*A list of titles in this series is available
at the end of the book.*

Cover Painting: The Museum of Fine Arts, Houston, The Bayou
Bend Collection, museum purchase funded by M. Robert Dussler,
D. Cal McNair, Ray Childress, Scott Schwinger, Dr. C. Thomas Caskey,
Malcolm Gillis, Wm. P. O'Connell, Chris Kersey, and Walter E. Johnson
in honor of Robert C. McNair and the Houston Texans at
"One Great Night in November, 2003", B.2003.

CONTENTS

Color illustrations follow page 76.

FOREWORD

The study of history involves a peculiar process of simultaneous recollecting and forgetting. The past is so vast that none of us can ever know it all. The best we can do is identify certain key features—in the words of the English writer Lytton Strachey, to "row out over that great ocean of material, and lower down into it, here and there, a little bucket, which will bring up to the light of day some characteristic specimen from those far depths." Yet, ironically, this same act relegates other facets of the past to obscurity, for attaching historical significance to certain topics implies that others can be allowed to slumber in the depths, undisturbed.

Every now and then, however, the tectonic plates undergirding our understanding of the past shift, causing historians to reassess the decisions of their predecessors. The recent efflorescence of scholarship in Native American history represents one such moment. Indigenous communities, of course, had always recognized the import of their history. But within the academy, it is only within the past quarter century that historians have realized that rather than minor actors, confined to a separate "prehistory" or "ethnohistory," American Indians are in fact foundational to many of the central questions of US history, from the rise of capitalism to the writing of the Constitution to the formulation of an American national identity.

Yet even as the understanding of Native history has expanded, certain blind spots linger. In the case of the Apache, Geronimo looms so large he eclipses most other aspects of his people's history. Known among his community as Guyaleé or "The Yawner," Geronimo was just one of the thousands of Apaches, divided into scores of distinct bands, attempting to preserve their way of life in the face of a relentlessly expanding United States. While noted among his fellow Chiricahua Apaches for his spiritual prowess, Geronimo never occupied a position of political authority, unlike such leaders as Mangas Coloradas, Cochise, or Victorio. Yet thanks to his status as the individual whose surrender in 1886 marks the formal end of the "Indian wars" in the United States, Geronimo has achieved an outsized influence on American culture. Geronimo's mystique received an added boost from the dramatic photos C. S. Fly took of him in his hideout in the Sierra Madre in the 1880s and his equally riveting autobiography, which he dictated in Spanish to the white educator, S. M. Barrett, while in captivity in Oklahoma in the early 1900s.

Even today, more than a century after his death, this popular fascination with Geronimo shows no signs of abating. Rumor has it that six years after Geronimo passed away in 1909, members of Skull and Bones, the elite Yale secret society, looted his grave in Fort Sill and smuggled his skull back to their tomb-like clubhouse in New Haven for use in their initiation rituals. US paratroopers began to use Geronimo's name as a battle cry during World War II, reportedly after watching a late-night screening of the 1939 Paramount Studios film, *Geronimo: The Story of a Great Enemy*. Following 9/11, Geronimo started to appear on t-shirts declaring "Homeland Security: Fighting Terrorism since 1492," for sale everywhere from powwows to Walmart. Most infamously, when members of Seal Team Six killed Osama Bin Laden in his hideout in Abbottabad, Pakistan, in 2011, they referenced Geronimo in the coded message announcing the completion of their mission: "Geronimo EKIA [Enemy Killed In Action]."

Geronimo, of course, should not be held responsible for such subsequent uses—and abuses—of his image. But the net effect of Americans' obsession with Guyaleé has been to obscure much of the rest of Apache history. One of the many virtues of the book that you hold in your hands is that it directs long-overdue attention toward the lesser-known Western Apache. A community distinct from Geronimo's Chiricahuas, the

Western Apache speak a unique dialect, follow separate cultural practices, and inhabit their own specific homeland in what would today be Arizona. The pages that follow also introduce a new cast of characters from those peopling most histories of the Apache, exemplified by the man into whose family the author married, Capitan Chiquito.

Capitan Chiquito's story is inseparable from the place he was born and endeavored to remain throughout his life, Aravaipa Canyon. A lush oasis amid an otherwise austere desert, Aravaipa possesses a natural beauty that belies its history as a site of repeated conflicts between the Western Apache—especially the bands known as T'iisibaan ("Cottonwoods in Gray Wedge Shape People" or Pinal Apache) and Tsézhiné ("Black Rocks People" or Aravaipa Apache)—and a shifting array of O'odham, Spanish, Mexican, and American rivals. Capitan Chiquito had the misfortune to be an eyewitness to the single bloodiest event to take place in the canyon: the "Camp Grant Massacre" of 1871, in which vigilantes from Tucson surrounded a camp of sleeping Apaches and murdered as many as 144 of them, including two of Capitan Chiquito's wives.

Given the genocidal violence that the United States directed toward Apaches in the nineteenth century, Capitan Chiquito was far from alone in seeing friends and family members killed by outsiders. But in the aftermath of the massacre, he made several remarkable decisions. Despite being forced onto the newly recreated San Carlos Apache Reservation (the same place where John Hartman would end up living and working close to a century later), Capitan Chiquito eventually returned to Aravaipa, establishing a homestead that included the very area where the massacre had taken place. How he coped with inhabiting a locale haunted by the deaths of so many of his people remains a mystery, especially given Apache traditions about avoiding contact with the deceased. But Capitan Chiquito's return to Aravaipa represented a powerful assertion: in spite of the violent acts of outsiders, the canyon remained Apache land. Capitan Chiquito and his family developed a small irrigated farm in Aravaipa. By the 1910s, this plot had become the nucleus for an Apache resettlement of the canyon that encompassed camps strung out for several miles along the canyon floor. Other Apaches from San Carlos paid temporary visits to these sites to see friends or relatives, expanding the Apache presence in Aravaipa even further.

It was during one of Capitan Chiquito's periodic journeys to Tucson to sell fruit from his orchard in Aravaipa that he undertook what may have been his most extraordinary act: a rapprochement with Jesús María Elías. In 1871, Elías had served as a guide for the attackers who committed the Camp Grant Massacre, making him responsible for the death of Capitan Chiquito's wives along with scores of the Apache's followers and extended family members. Not only did Capitan Chiquito stay from time to time at the Elías house in Tucson; when he remarried, Elías gave him a horse and saddle, along with a collection of brightly colored calico dresses for his new wife. For his part, Capitan Chiquito reciprocated by gifting Elías with a cane covered with blue and white beads—possibly the same sort of cane used in the Western Apache Sunrise Ceremony and meant to symbolize long life.

Once one learns about such exceptional aspects of Capitan Chiquito's life, it becomes hard not to conclude that one of the reasons why non-Natives have been so quick to celebrate Geronimo's story while ignoring Capitan Chiquito's is that the latter poses a number of disturbing questions they would just as soon ignore. In an odd way, Geronimo remains so famous because his stubborn resistance to US expansion aligns with certain stereotypes justifying US conquest. Geronimo's history can be taken to suggest that there was no way for Apaches and whites to avoid violence in their interactions with one another—indeed, Geronimo's repeated escapes from the reservation, each of which left a bloody conflict in its wake, could be seen as implying that much of this violence originated with the Apaches themselves. From this perspective, Geronimo's ultimate surrender and subsequent exile from his homeland may inspire a certain nostalgic sense of loss, but they also emerge as the necessary cost of peace.

In contrast, it is far harder to interpret Capitan Chiquito in such a simplistic and misguided manner. The fact that Capitan Chiquito lived out his days in relative tranquility in the same canyon where his people suffered a devastating massacre should cause us to reassess who, in fact, was responsible for the brutal confrontations between Apaches and non-Natives that occurred with frightening regularity throughout the nineteenth century. Likewise, that Capitan Chiquito was able to reconcile with one of the individuals most responsible for a terrible atrocity against his people speaks volumes about the capacity of Apache forms of justice to address past wrongs in a pacific manner—and reminds us that outsiders have seldom acknowledged the validity of such practices. Even the mere fact that Capitan Chiquito regularly marketed his produce in Tucson undercuts any notion of a fundamental incompatibility between

Natives and modern life, while also highlighting that Apache history did not end in 1886 with Geronimo's surrender but instead continued along its own unique trajectory in the years afterward.

Through his marriage to Velma Bullis, Capitan Chiquito's great-granddaughter, John Hartman gained rare access to the oral traditions that preserved a detailed knowledge of this past yet never made it into the history books. Such oral traditions are especially important for a group like the Apache. Outsiders, most of them deeply hostile to the people they were writing about, produced the overwhelming majority of the primary documents on the Apache that have ended up in the archive. All too often, subsequent historians have uncritically incorporated the biases embedded in these sources into their scholarship, producing works that offer a distorted image of the Apaches. Even in the nineteenth century, the Western Apache leader Hashke Bahnzin ("Angry, Men Stand in Line for Him"), like Capitan Chiquito a survivor of the Camp Grant Massacre, critiqued this asymmetry, observing that whites "write for the papers and tell their own story. The Apache have no one to tell their story."

It will take more than one book to correct such imbalances. By last count, there are close to 700 biographies of Geronimo in print. This current volume, in contrast, is the first biography of Capitan Chiquito. Moreover, unlike the authors writing about Geronimo, Hartman did not have the luxury of an autobiography to work from but instead had to piece together a portrait of Capitan Chiquito from scattered fragments. Alongside this portrait, Hartman has interwoven background material on Apache history as well as a memoir of his time in San Carlos living with Capitan Chiquito's descendants. The resulting narrative traces the dislocations caused by American settler colonialism across multiple generations of a single family from the nineteenth century up to the current moment. At once academic, deeply personal, and altogether unforgettable, it represents a unique introduction to the past and present of the Western Apache.

—*Karl Jacoby*

Allan Nevins Professor of American History
Department of History and Center
for the Study of Ethnicity and Race
Columbia University
New York, New York

ACKNOWLEDGMENTS

I owe much gratitude to my departed father-in-law, Lonnie Bullis, for my first introduction to Capitan Chiquito, who was his grandfather. Lonnie did not talk much of his past, but he left me some jewels of information on occasion, as I lived with him the last seven years of his life.

I can't remember how I first made contact with Allan Radbourne of the English Westerners Society, but he became one of my mentors in the understanding of Apache history. Even though he lived in England, he knew much more about the Apaches than I did even though I lived on the Apache reservation. I identify much with Allan because we are both amateur historians. He spent about thirty years of his life researching his book on Mickey Free, and I spent about the same amount of time researching Capitan Chiquito. My correspondence with Allan was always by email, and I just missed meeting him once when he came to the Apache Cultural Center in 2005 and he did not realize that I lived next door to that place. Allan gave me almost all the information I have on Capitan Chiquito's various enlistments as an Apache scout. Allan passed away in 2019 and I'm sorry I cannot give him a copy of my Capitan Chiquito story.

My research hit a gold mine in 2008 with the publication of Karl Jacoby's *Shadows at Dawn* and Ian Record's *Big Sycamore Stands Alone*. I became friends with both of these authors on their visits to San Carlos. My wife and I shared some information on Aravaipa with Ian, but he shared much more with me as he researched his book and gave me various letters and articles on the life of Capitan Chiquito. The Shadows at Dawn website that was posted after the publication of Karl Jacoby's book provided me with a wealth of information on Capitan Chiquito in the Documents section. Historical research reminds me of archaeological excavation, but instead of digging in the earth you are digging into mounds of documents and the books of others who leave you clues of information.

Another one of my mentors on Apache culture through the years is the ethnobotanist Seth Pilsk of the San Carlos Apache Forestry Department. Seth has worked for over twenty-five years with the Elders of the San Carlos Apaches in documenting the Apache names of the trees, herbs, valleys, mountains, and rivers of the ancient Apache land. I asked him several times to give presentations on Apache culture to our hospital staff.

Stevenson Talgo, who works in the Map Room of the San Carlos Forestry Department, created all the maps I am using in this story. Thank you very much Stevenson, who usually goes by the name of Dobson Talgo.

I am thankful to Ross Blair, the great-grandson of the commanding officer at Camp Grant, First Lieutenant Royal Whitman. Ross shared with me several passages from his ancestor's journal that gave much better insight into the personality of Capitan Chiquito. Ross also read my whole manuscript and helped me with editing. The great-grandson of Juan Elias, a nemesis of Capitan Chiquito but later a friend, also shared some fascinating stories that helped me to better understand the viewpoint of the people of Tucson on the Apache people. His name is Ramon Elias.

Two other people who have read my book and helped me with spelling errors and grammar errors are Phil Hendrick and Theresa Brunton. Phil is a retired geneticist who lives in Aravaipa Canyon and has done research on bighorn sheep, Mexican wolves, and other endangered species. Theresa is the wife of an Orthodox priest who lives at the Saint Paisius Orthodox Monastery near Safford, Arizona, where my wife is buried.

If I have any ability to write creatively and to put my feelings into written words, I want to give credit to my high school English teacher Father Alton Carr of the Redemptorist Fathers. He, more than any subsequent college English professor I ever had, taught me how to write.

Thank you very much to all of you.

CAPITAN **CHIQUITO**

Introduction

WE BROUGHT HER SKULL back in January 2013. It had been sitting in a drawer at the Smithsonian Institution for 140 years, ever since Dr. Valery Havard picked it up from the massacre site and sent it back East. The skull was that of an Apache woman of twenty-five to thirty years old. Her skull was intact, so it had not been smashed in by Papago war clubs. She was probably shot or stabbed and, hopefully, not violated. When my wife died the following summer, I thought of the words of an elderly Apache lady at the tribal repatriation meetings: "You all are not even supposed to be talking about this! This is not the Apache way to be thinking of the dead, or to have anything to do with the bones of the dead!"

Yet another Apache woman related the story of a woman she met at a NAGPRA meeting in Albuquerque. NAGPRA is the Native American Grave Protection and Repatriation Act. This woman worked in the very room that many Apache bones and artifacts are held. One day she had an Ezekiel-like vision there. She said that the bones of the Apache people came together and told her, "We want to go back to 'Ni Te gochi.'" Ni Te gochi is the old Apache name for the San Carlos Apache Reservation.

I have much admiration for my departed wife's Apache heritage, especially since her great-grandfather was a well-known and revered

Apache chief. I did not even know that my wife was Apache when I fell in love with her many years ago in Los Angeles. When she finally agreed to marry me, we determined to come to the San Carlos Apache Reservation to take care of her father in his final years. I took a job with Indian Health Service in the San Carlos emergency room. My wife, Velma, worked with tribal social services. Her father was the grandson of Chief Capitan Chiquito, and he told me much about his grandfather. When he told me that his grandfather was in prison with Geronimo, I thought to myself, "Oh sure, everyone wants a Geronimo connection. Capitan Chiquito was not Chiricahua. This must be a family myth." I was later to discover that this myth was a reality.

About six months before Capitan Chiquito's grandson died, he pointed out the window on the south side of our home. He said, "Do you see those bare-breasted Apache maidens dancing there?" I said, "I'm sorry Lonnie. I wish I could, but I cannot." I later learned that Apache women only danced bare breasted in a victory dance when their men would return from a successful raid into Mexico.

I do not believe that I violated any Apache taboo for my part in returning this Apache lady's skull. An Apache medicine man once told me that this woman's spirit would never rest until her skull was brought back to the place of her murder. On a recent trip to the massacre site, I walked among the graves with one of Capitan Chiquito's great-grand-children from his son Joe. I always get a feeling of nausea when I walk there. It is a place of screams, rape, and murder. Not just one murder, but many. They were mostly women and children and babies.

My friend was speaking in Apache as we walked along and I asked her what it was that she was saying. She said that the spirits were asking her what we were doing here. She told them that we are here in respect of you and we want to see the place where Capitan Chiquito lived and died. The mesa of the massacre is overgrown with cholla cactus. You must be careful with every step or the spikes of a cactus ball can penetrate your shoe. They are sometimes called "jumping cactus," as you find them on your shirt or pants without even thinking that you touched one of them. The spirits told her that the mesa is covered with cholla cactus because they do not want to be disturbed.

There is much controversy about this place. It is thought to be haunted and is definitely a place where men have done evil to other men. There is an Apache saying that "wisdom sits in places." That is to say, that the land itself influences the events that take place on it, and the human events that take place on the land leave an everlasting imprint on it.

The young woman's skull that we returned that day was possibly one of Capitan Chiquito's wives. It is documented that he had one or two wives killed in the massacre that morning. I do not believe that my wife's death took place because we returned that young lady's remains, but I do believe in serendipity. There are "wheels within wheels" and "a time for every purpose under heaven." I feel that the return of my wife's ancestor was part of what she needed to accomplish to put closure on her life. The day that Velma became ill, I retired from the San Carlos emergency room after twenty-one years. There is nothing for me here in San Carlos now. It was an honor to serve the Apache tribe. I need to move on. Velma left the planet from the same west room and window of our home where her father left fourteen years before her. The sister of the medicine man, Phillip Cassadore, who brought the Sunrise Dance back to the San Carlos Reservation, once told me, "John, if you ever try to leave Apache land, I will sing you back! You are an Apache captive." Well, she has left now through that same western portal as my wife. It is time for me to leave here, and I pray to Usen, the Apache Father/Mother God, to guide me until the end of my life, and to give it purpose.

But before they will let me go, I have a story to tell.

How I Came to Live with the San Carlos Apaches

WHEN CAPITAN CHIQUITO'S GRANDSON, Lonnie Bullis, moved back to Arizona in 1973, his daughter, Velma, accompanied him to help with his move. Velma's friends at the time describe her as being somewhat of a party girl and flower child. Velma was an accomplished swimmer, ice skater, and skier. In Arizona her dad took her to visit some old friends in Aravaipa Canyon, which was the ancestral homeland of his Apache band. They visited the Woods family who had bought part of the Kielberg Ranch. The Kielbergs had left the canyon in 1925, saying that it held too many sad memories for them.[1] This visit to the canyon was the first time that Velma realized that her great-grandfather was an Apache chief. Much of Velma's family past was unknown to her but would gradually unfold like a fascinating mystery story. She surely would never have guessed that her last name of Bullis was the name of the man who sent her great-grandfather, Chiquito, to prison, but this is getting ahead of my story.

On Velma's first visit to Arizona her father took her to visit their ancestral homeland, and Velma fell in love with it. The drive to Aravaipa Canyon from Globe is about one hour. Globe is the closest town to the San Carlos Apache reservation on the west side and is where her father first moved on his return to Arizona. Lonnie introduced his daughter to Fred and Cliff Wood, who were Lonnie's boyhood friends from his early visits to Aravaipa. Lonnie had corresponded with them even in his years living in Iowa. They would sit and drink beer and talk while Velma went horseback riding into the canyon. Velma always liked to tell me the story of a horseback ride she took into the canyon with one of the Woods' boys who lived there. Velma invited him to go skinny dipping with her in a beautiful pool of water, and he said: "No, if my Pa ever found out, he would whip my butt."

After Velma returned to Chicago, her dad took an accounting job with H&R Block in Globe. Through friends in Globe, Lonnie made a connection with a forty-three-year-old woman in the Philippines and began a correspondence. At the age of sixty-seven Lonnie flew to the Philippines and married her in September 1974. The following year Lonnie obtained employment with the Bureau of Indian Affairs Finance Loan Department, and Lonnie and his new wife, Theresa "Tessie" Surat, moved to Main Street in San Carlos. They lived for many years in the tufa stone house that is now the Tribal Wellness Center. Tessie was a hard-working woman and became well-liked in the community. She made and sold food of all kinds and is known today as the person who started the food vending service at Geronimo Square in San Carlos.

In the same September that her dad married Tessie, Velma flabbergasted her friends by joining a religious order in Chicago. Velma had never seemed religious to her friends. She was not exactly "wild," as Chiquito's son Alonzo described himself before his conversion, but this change seemed very different from the Velma her friends knew. I had joined this same group in New Orleans in 1971. I had gone to a Roman Catholic minor seminary and had become disenchanted with Catholicism. I read mostly metaphysical and occult literature while attending college in New Orleans. I dropped out of college and joined this group at the age of nineteen after speaking to a priest from this order, who seemed to have a tangible mystical presence. This religious order was founded in the Haight-Ashbury district of San Francisco in 1968 by a man known to his followers as Father Paul. Father Paul converted many a hippie to his version of Christianity. Outwardly, we dressed as Catholic clergy and had a similar liturgy, but we also taught reincarnation and astrology; our mission was to "Unite all Faiths," and to show the underlying truths at the core of each religion. We thought we were going to save the world.

I first met Velma when I was a minister in this order in Los Angeles in 1976. Velma was sent there, and well, love is destiny. I was sent out of the order by the director of the order for "spending too much time with Velma to the detriment of my ministry." When Velma went to San Carlos on vacation to visit her father in 1977, I visited San Carlos for the first time. I remember going out with Velma to the Seven Mile District somewhere on the reservation at night and lying on a blanket under the stars in July. I guess God protects fools, because we were not stung by scorpions, bitten by rattlesnakes, or assaulted like many of the people I would later see in the San Carlos emergency room who were foolish enough to be out after dark.

Velma left the order the following August to join me in Houston. We planned on marrying, but Velma decided to return to that group after two months of living with me. She told me that "I was the right person at the wrong time." I was devastated. I did not see or hear from her again for fourteen years.

In 1981 Lonnie Bullis sold his father's land in Aravaipa Canyon. He had wanted to build a home there but could not afford the cost of drilling a well, connecting electricity, then building a house. Lonnie used the money from the sale to build a home in Peridot near the present Apache Cultural Center. Peridot is one of the three communities on the reservation with its own post office, the other two being San Carlos and Bylas. The land they built their home on was a barren plain, but with a great view of Mount Turnbull, Triplet Mountain, and Peridot Hill. Peridot Hill is the only place in the United States where peridot is mined. The hill is actually the caldera of an ancient volcano that spewed peridot from the guts of the earth a half million years ago. It is a green semiprecious stone that the Apaches still mine with pick and shovel on the volcanic mesa that it formed. Lonnie and Tessie turned this barren plain into what some Apaches refer to today as "the Jungle."

Tessie planted many palm trees to remind her of her homeland. Lonnie planted pines, cedars, cottonwood trees, and cacti of all sorts. He had two grape arbors and a large blackberry patch. Lonnie inherited his green thumb from his grandfather, Chiquito, who was well known for the beautiful and bountiful orchard and gardens he cultivated in Aravaipa Canyon. Capitan Chiquito's knowledge and abilities about growing plants was how he was able to keep six wives. Chiquito's son, Alonzo, was also a gifted agriculturist and once had a farm in Old San Carlos.

Chiquito's grandson, Lonnie, always planted a garden, even in his years in Iowa. Lonnie told me once how his father had kicked him and had never given him anything in his life. I reminded Lonnie that his dad taught him how to make things grow and had once given him a horse.

Lonnie's wife, Tessie, started a restaurant next door to their home called the Peridot Restaurant in the building that is now the Apache Cultural Center. Lonnie retired from the Bureau of Indian Affairs about this time after nine years, yet he did income tax returns for the Apache community into his late eighties. Lonnie told me that he ran for tribal councilman for his district at this time. Before a gathering of potential Apache voters, he attempted to speak Apache to the best of his ability, and they laughed at him. It really hurt his feelings. He had been away a long time.

After Velma's departure from my life, I returned to California and married an old friend who I ran into again in San Francisco. I went back to school and eventually obtained a license as a registered nurse and naturopathic physician in Portland, Oregon. Velma lived most of that time in Forestville, California, at the order's headquarters and retreat center. The directors of the order made her the nanny for their children and sent her to Michigan for training in the Waldorf Institute to learn more about the education of children. She eventually began to train others in the order as schoolteachers and was a key figure in starting Saint Michael's School, which became the model for the education of children throughout the order's centers.

When Velma died, the sisters placed an icon (religious painting) of Saint Michael on her chest. It is buried with her to commemorate her part in founding this school. The directors of the order wanted to move the group into something more mainstream and acceptable in the Christian world. In 1988 Velma was baptized in the Eastern Orthodox Christian Church, as was most of the rest of the order. A few years after this change occurred, Velma left her clerical garbs behind and moved to Santa Barbara, California, to begin working on a master's degree in psychology.

I decided to call Velma on her fortieth birthday, at about the time she was making this transition, and we began to correspond. I had raised a stepson and had three children of my own. I was studying anthropology at Texas A&M University in College Station, Texas, and was fascinated with Native Americans. I invited Velma to meet me in Albuquerque,

New Mexico, and then drive to the awesome Ancestral Puebloan ruins at Chaco Canyon. It was our first meeting in fourteen years.

I had no problems with my wife and I did love her, but there is a difference between loving a person and being "crazy" about someone. I think crazy has to do with destiny and perhaps karmic ties from the distant past. I started to see a psychologist to sort out my thoughts and feelings. I had a stable life, a good job, loved my children, and I lived close to my parents and siblings. Well, crazy won out. I completed my bachelor's degree in anthropology at Texas A&M and moved to San Carlos in November 1992.

Velma's dad, Lonnie, was eighty-five when I moved in with him. He had divorced Tessie the same year. Velma was completing her master of arts degree in psychology in Santa Barbara and did not join us until the following summer. Getting to know Lonnie was not an easy process. He just saw me as a usurper. His landscaping had deteriorated quite a bit since Tessie left, and I started to work on the place to save the trees he had planted and to plant some trees of my own. He kind of mocked my "good intentions" and always suspected that I was just there to take over his place.

I worked for the Indian Health Service in the emergency room of the San Carlos Apache Hospital. All of the non-Apache employees would stay in the apartments on the government compound, which was land that the Apache tribe designated for hospital workers that were not tribal members. Since Velma was a member of the San Carlos Apache tribe, I was allowed to live on the reservation in their home in the tribal district of Peridot. When Velma joined us, she was employed as a counselor with Tribal Social Services. She eventually became the manager of the Tribal Youth Home, a place where the tribe placed children without parents or who had been taken from their parents.

Although Velma never had any children of her own, she was good with children and had specialized in early childhood development. While Velma worked at the youth home we got to know an eight-year-old girl named Melissa Dudley. Her mom had died in a car accident. I will always remember the first time I met her. She hung her head sadly and said, "I have child abuse," as if it is a disease that you contract (and I suppose she was right). We were later asked to be Melissa's godparents at an Apache Sunrise Dance, which is an initiation done when a young girl comes into puberty. Melissa would play a big role in our life drama, which I will speak of later.

Lonnie's daughter, Deana, had never visited Arizona until 1987.

When Ian Record was researching his book *Big Sycamore Stands Alone*, he came to our home in the Peridot district of the Apache reservation. At this time Ian was senior lecturer for American Indian studies at the University of Arizona.

Record quotes Velma and her sister Deana Reed in his book: "Up until that time I'd never heard of Aravaipa," says Reed, who lives with her family in Moline, Illinois. "I hadn't made the connection between our family and the canyon. Daddy was always so close-mouthed about everything. He was a storehouse of information, most of which he took to his grave." During her first visit, Deana says, her father "did talk about going to visit Chiquito as a child. One time, his horse ate too much grass and got bloated. They tried to poke a hole in the horse's stomach to relieve the pressure, but it didn't work, and the horse died. My father also expressed outrage at the desecration of the graves of his relatives and the other Apaches who are buried there."[2]

According to both daughters, their father's reunion with Arapa during his twilight years gave him the chance not only to revisit his roots and his past but also to make peace with the conflicts and contradictions in his life. "He was between two worlds—the white man's world and the Indian's world. He didn't fit into either one comfortably," says Velma, adding that her father's reservation upbringing, his "traumatic" Lutheran boarding school experiences, and his mixed-blood heritage made for a "paradoxical life."[3]

In my first few years living on the reservation, I was often greeted by passers-by with "F you, you white people! This is our land!" My hiking buddy, Jon Walker, had similar experiences when he first moved to the reservation. He lived in a trailer-home park on San Carlos Lake where the Apache tribe allowed non-Apaches to live. He was at the San Carlos Lake store and an Apache man thought he was staring at him and said, "What are you looking at?" Jon said, "Oh. I'm just buying some beer. I live right over there on the lakeside." The Apache man replied, "You may stay here, but you don't live here."

I have much admiration for Jon's wife, Juliet Benvenuto. She lived with Velma and me for a while when she first came to the reservation.

Velma helped her establish herself here, and she first obtained employment with Tribal Social Services; she has worked for them to this day.

I have much respect for any nurse or nurse assistant who could work in the San Carlos emergency room for over a year. People sometimes see them as calloused, but they all have hearts of gold and a commitment to the community. If you would let every experience there into your heart, you would never stop crying. Working in the San Carlos emergency room was like living in a fishbowl. I would sometimes drive to the hospital to begin my shift and seeing the parking lot full of cars with patients waiting to be seen, I would want to turn around and drive home. I developed somewhat of a cool and calm demeaner. When every day you deal with crisis after crisis, there is not much that can make you anxious. There are some emergency room doctors and nurses who love the thrill and adrenal rush of an emergency, but this was not me. I found that if I was getting excited, anxious, or "hyper" about the situation that I was not functioning at my best. Our emergency room staff worked hard to be prepared for any crisis that walked through our doors.

I was soon a well-known figure in the community of 15,000. I remember one elderly Apache man who came into the emergency room and looked at me and started to laugh. I had long hair and a beard then. He said, "Now I know what my grandson meant when he told me that Jesus gave him a shot."

I cannot talk in great detail about my experiences in the San Carlos emergency room because of federal confidentiality laws. But it is a well-known fact that the major triad of problems facing the Apaches has to do with the drastic changes in their diet and lifestyle that occurred when they were placed in the "San Carlos Concentration Camp" (as some Apaches call the reservation) and given government rations: that triad is diabetes, obesity, and alcoholism.

I had worked about ten years with patients in intensive care units before coming to the reservation. I had seen much but had never seen anything so frightening and anxiety provoking as a young child stung by a scorpion. They look as if they are "possessed by the devil" with eyes darting back and forth, copious salivation, and thrashing about inconsolably. A scorpion sting can be fatal to a child. I am happy for the part I played in coordinating research for a new scorpion antivenom. Our emergency room was one of the sites that was authorized to provide this remedy. This intravenous medicine became the first drug approved by the FDA that is made in Mexico. Formerly we would have to fly the child out on a ventilator but can now send them home within three hours. I imagine the Apache people in the past lost many a child to this venomous creature.

We would treat on the average about one rattlesnake bite a year. I remember one intoxicated man who came in after trying to pick up a rattlesnake. He had grabbed it behind its head, but it turned and managed to get one fang in his hand. The small lesion in his hand was not too impressive, but when I saw him a week or so later his whole arm was black. The surgeons had to make a cut from his wrist to his shoulder so the swelling would not cause permanent nerve damage.

We trained to be ready for anything that walked through the doors. I always wondered what I might do if a person arrived with a Gila monster clamped on their arm or leg. When these creatures bite you they don't let go. I had read of a case where a motorcyclist had fallen into a ditch and had a Gila monster clamp onto his hand. Another recorded case was a man who had parachuted out of a plane. As the desert winds dragged him across the mesa, a Gila monster latched on to his shoulder.[4] The medical literature says to try dunking it under water or lighting a flame under its jaw to make it let go. I thought the best thing to try would be an injection of pancuronium. This drug was derived from the poison used on blow gun darts in South America to drop monkeys from the trees, as it completely paralyzed the nervous system. We used it to paralyze people who needed to be placed on a ventilator.

Velma's dad, Lonnie, actually got to like me toward the end of his life. He would always tell me very sincerely, "Thank you, John," when I shaved him or helped him with his bath. In 1999 Lonnie took a fall in our kitchen and broke his pelvis. He never stood again and he died in our home on hospice at the age of ninety-two. I was awakened that September morning by a large gust of wind from the east that raised our curtains high in the air. When I went to check on him, I found that his spirit had been sent soaring out of our west window. According to his wishes, his body was cremated and buried on our property on ground consecrated by Father Gino, the Franciscan priest at the San Carlos Catholic Church.

Because of Lonnie and his life experience, I developed a great interest in Aravaipa Canyon. I held several meetings with the landowners, all who were descendants of Capitan Chiquito. Chiquito was able to gain ownership of the 160 acres where the infamous Camp Grant Massacre took place. The general consensus of the group was that they never wanted to sell the land, but they wished to return it to the natural state of beauty that it had one hundred years ago. They were against placing any kind of historical marker there to memorialize the massacre victims, until the land could be properly fenced and protected from intruders.

I also began to research how to have the skull of the Apache woman returned to Aravaipa, which was taken from the site by Dr. Valery Havard. I found the Smithsonian Institution staff to be very cooperative. They said to just get a letter from the chairman requesting the remains, and they would pay to fly two people to Washington, DC, to claim them. The tribal chairman wanted us to get a consensus of the Aravaipa clan on whether or not to request the return of the remains. I was somewhat surprised that the return of her remains would be so controversial. After all, who would want their great-grandmother's remains in a museum? Yet the Apache way of thinking is different from that of the white man.

According to anthropologist Keith Basso, "Most Western Apaches hold firmly to the understanding that talking about trouble and adversity can increase the chances of its occurrence. Consequently, when speaking about themselves or others, they avoid making statements that suggest or allude to the possibility of misfortune, especially sickness and death. In contradistinction, Anglo-Americans are observed to speak about such matters often and in what Apaches regard as a supremely casual fashion, a practice that gives rise to the bizarre impression that white men are eager to experience hardship and disaster."[5]

After four public meetings and some very heated discussions, the clan agreed that the remains should be returned. They wanted no public ceremony, but they requested that one medicine man return the remains discretely with proper ceremony. In January 2013, Velma and I went with Seth Pilsk of the Apache Elders Council to bring the remains to the home of Lyman Priest Bullis. Lyman is the medicine man who was chosen to bury the remains. He is a great-grandchild of Capitan Chiquito, as Velma is.

Velma was a deeply religious and spiritual lady. She dragged me by my ear to church every Sunday to the Saint Paisius Orthodox Christian Monastery near Safford, Arizona. When Velma became ill, I left my job as nursing supervisor of the San Carlos emergency room. I had worked there twenty-one years and had seen a generation of Apache children grow from infancy to adulthood. Velma was eventually placed on hospice. Two priests and two sisters from the monastery came out to our home to administer last rites to Velma. She died peacefully the next day on the first of August with her sister, Deana, and me at her bedside. The sisters from the monastery prepared her body for burial and she was buried at the monastery on August 6. I feel that I was touched by someone with a special relationship with the divine, or "star power" as the Apaches might say.

San Carlos is not an easy place to raise a son who is non-Apache. I hiked almost every mountain on the San Carlos Reservation with my son Lucas to keep him out of trouble. One of our most memorial hikes was our climb to the summit of Mount Turnbull. Mount Turnbull is in the Santa Theresa Mountains and at 8,284 feet, it is the highest mountain on the reservation. The Apache call the mountain Ch'ishdlaazhe and it is one of their most sacred mountains. General Miles used this mountain as one of his heliograph sites when he set up heliograph stations all over Arizona. A team of soldiers would signal with mirrors from mountaintop to mountaintop over great distances in the campaign to find Geronimo. The telegraph lines were often useless in this mountainous terrain, and the Apache would often cut these lines then tie them together with rawhide to make the break in the line difficult to find. I climbed this mountain with my eleven-year-old son, and he always remembers how I left him alone on a rock ledge near the summit to make sure the summit was safe. I probably left him alone for less than a minute, yet it was quite frightening to him because he thought I might have fallen off the other side.

When my son returned from his first tour of Afghanistan as a marine infantryman, his radioman told me that their team attributed their survival to his hiking and orienteering skills. Their team of four would basically go out as "bait" for the Taliban. When they started to be shot at, they would call out the Taliban positions to soldiers from the air force. My son said that Afghanistan reminded him of San Carlos.

I will miss San Carlos and the Apache people, but, of course, I miss Velma the most. It is so strange that a person you love can "disappear." You can never hear them, hold them, or see them again. I wrote this story as a gift to Velma and her sister, Deana, and as a therapy for myself. If I did not write it down, it would be lost. I had researched and collected information on the life of Capitan Chiquito for years. After Velma died I spent a year living alone in our house on the reservation to finish this book and was determined not to leave until it was done. There are many more stories just as fascinating as the life of Capitan Chiquito. Apache history is not all about Geronimo. I would love to read the stories of chiefs such as Talkalai, Cassadore, Nosey, and others.

I have left San Carlos now, and my Apache godchild, Melissa, and family live in the home where Velma and I stayed for twenty-one years. I know she will take care of the trees that Lonnie and his wife planted, and that Velma and I planted. Lonnie's daughter, Deana, and I took Lonnie's remains from our property in Peridot and buried them near his grandfather, Chiquito, in Aravaipa Canyon. I think that I can only say like Lonnie said when he was sent away to boarding school: I will never forget the Apache. I will never forget the Apache. I will never forget the Apache.

The Invasion of Apache Lands by the Spanish Empire

"ARISE, ABRAHAM, THE DAY of judgment has come!" By these words Lincoln was awakened by his mother on the night of November 13, 1833. Lincoln and his mother were eyewitnesses to the great Leonid meteor shower. Lincoln related this story to his advisers during the darkest days of the Civil War when they feared that the union was lost. The president wisely commented, "Gentlemen, the world did not come to an end then, nor will the union now."[1]

During the four hours that preceded dawn on November 13, 1833, the skies were lit up by thousands of shooting stars every minute. Newspapers of that era reveal that almost no one was unaware of the shower. If they were not alerted by the cries of their excited neighbors, they were usually awakened by flashes of light cast into normally dark bedrooms by the fireballs.

This event was significant in the life of Capitan Chiquito, as he related that he was about twelve years old when this celestial phenomenon occurred, making the year of his birth 1821.[2] This was the same year that Mexico won its independence from Spain. Spain had claimed the land of Chiquito's birth ever since the Coronado expedition of 1540. They claimed the land, but they never conquered it. The Apache were to become the greatest challenge in Spain's expansion north into Indian lands. One great gift that the Spanish brought to the Apache was the horse. The Apache called the horse "the Gift of the Gods." Before the Apache acquired the horse in their war with Spain, they traveled over the earth with their possessions on their backs or on teams of pack dogs.

The Indians of Acoma and the Pueblo Indians of Albuquerque were in awe when they first saw the horses of the Spanish soldiers. It is recorded that these tribes smeared themselves with the sweat of this amazing and unknown animal.[3] Perhaps they wanted to transfer the strength and magic of this wonderful creature to themselves. Yet when Coronado's soldiers first encountered the buffalo hunting Apache along the Canadian River in the Texas panhandle, it is written in Pedro de Castaneda's account that they displayed curiosity about the Spanish horses but did not seem to be disturbed by them in the least.[4] Southwestern folklorist LaVerne Harrell Clark comments:

> Perhaps their reactions were a sign predicting the early Apache mastery of the horse, for unlike the Pueblo Indians of New Mexico, who were the first southwest Indians to acquire horses in sizable numbers, the Apache and their Navaho relatives were the first to develop into a real horse people.[5]

The Spanish did not realize that they had kicked a hornet's nest by their invasion of these northern lands. It would take a couple of generations for the Apache to master the horse and acquire horses in large numbers, but they would eventually invade the Spanish missions and ranches in hordes and avenge the war crimes and atrocities that the Spanish soldiers had inflicted on Zuni, Acoma, and the pueblos of Albuquerque. Among the Spanish atrocities was the burning at the stake of one hundred Pueblo warriors near Albuquerque by one of Coronado's officers, Don Garcia de Cardenas. When these warriors surrendered and asked for peace, Cardenas had his men prepare two hundred stakes to burn them alive.

In Castaneda's account of the event, he writes:

> Thus when the enemies saw that their comrades were being tied and that the Spaniards had started to burn them, about one hundred who were in the tent began to offer resistance and defend themselves with what they found about them and with stakes that which they rushed out to seize.

These Indians were all killed by Spanish horsemen as they ran to escape across the open plains.[6]

If it were not for the migration of the Apaches from the Pacific Northwest to the Southwest about a century before Columbus, the history of the Southwest would have gone much more favorably for the Spanish. The Apache were a nomadic Athabascan speaking tribe that knew how to live off the land.

I like to learn new languages and can read Latin, French, and Spanish fairly well, yet I found learning Apache to be a great challenge. After taking Apache 101 twice at the Apache Community College, I could speak a few short sentences, such as asking someone if their stomach hurt who came to the emergency room. *"Ya bid nnii ne?"* Apache is a "tonal" language and not one of the so-called Romance languages. Later in my life I am becoming quiet fluent in Mandarin Chinese, which I find similar to Apache but actually easier for me to understand. Yet this is a story that I will include in my epilogue.

Most Apaches today are comfortable with speaking English, but there are some elders who do not speak or understand English. I learned much about Apache culture from my friend Seth Pilsk, a botanist who has worked with the tribal elders for many years. One of his efforts is the Apache Place Names Project, where he is documenting the Apache names for every mountain, creek, plant, animal, and other natural features of the land that was once theirs. Seth once told me that in a conversation with some Hopi elders, he was told that when the Hopi first saw the Apache wandering through their land they said that they did not know if they were men or animals. The Apache looked and moved so "at one" with nature that it made them "a creature apart" from other men.[7]

Another bane for the Spanish was the migration of the Comanche tribe into Texas following the Apache. The Comanche were to become even better horsemen than the Apache, and they eventually drove the Apache west into Arizona. You do not hear of the Hopi, Zuni, and Pueblo Indians invading Spanish territory. They had occupied the southwest for centuries and had a lifestyle centered in their villages. The Comanche would begin to raid the Spanish settlements south of Texas and New Mexico, and the Apache would raid the Spanish from New Mexico and Arizona.

The historian John Upton Terrel writes:

> The 17th century was not very old when the Spanish gave up hope of preventing Indians from acquiring horses. The situation was far beyond possible to control, and they concentrated their efforts on the most important—but in itself extremely difficult—task of staying alive under the burden of almost constant raids made upon them.[8]

Herbert Eugene Bolton writes on this same subject. Bolton was an American historian who pioneered the study of the Spanish-American borderlands. He writes in his biography of the Jesuit missionary Francisco Kino:

> When first heard of, the Apaches, though warlike, covered a narrow range and were devoted somewhat to agriculture. But the Spaniards brought horses to the frontier, the Apaches acquired them, and their range widened. The Spanish had also vast herds of cattle which the Apache came to prize as food. In other words, the Spaniards raise stock and at the same time gave the Apaches the means of stealing it. As the 17th century waned, the raids became longer and longer, until by Kino's day the Apaches not only ravaged border missions and outlying ranches, but penetrated the very heart of Sonora, supplementing theft with fire and murder. The blame was not one sided. Spanish soldiery pursued the invaders, slew the warriors when they could catch them, captured women and children and kept them as slaves.[9]

I don't believe the Apache were anymore naturally "warlike," as Bolton says, than the Spanish. After all, it was the Spanish who had first invaded Apache territory. If it were not for the Spanish invasion of their lands, they would probably not have developed their raiding and warfare culture. Although they were described by the Coronado expedition as "better proportioned, greater warriors, and more feared" than the Pueblo Indians, it was also stated, "They are gentle people, not cruel, and are faithful in their friendship."[10]

By 1770 the Spanish had developed a policy of dealing with the Apaches once and for all, or so they thought. Mark Santiago writes in graphic detail of the cruelty of the Spanish policy to the Apache in his book *The Jar of Severed Hands*. In explaining this policy, he writes:

> This called for individual Apache rancherias to be settled near Spanish Presidios on what later historians would call establecimientos de paz— peace establishments. Here the Apaches would be given food, clothing,

and other supplies in exchange for stopping their raids against Spanish settlements. Apache men would be enlisted to serve as scouts and auxiliaries against those rancherias that refused to accept that offer, and they would be rewarded for their service with horses, weapons, and other gifts. Apache women and children would be encouraged to coexist with their new Hispanic neighbors and to adopt their habits, and their vices—including learning agricultural techniques, attending school, and gambling at cards. For those Apaches who refused the Spanish offer, the alternative was stark: they would be hunted down and killed and those captured would be transported from their homelands for ever.[11]

Hundreds of Apaches were marched in chains from the borderlands to Mexico City. Those who survived were then marched to Veracruz, placed on ships, and sent to Cuba to work as slaves in the fields. The deportation of Apache prisoners of war came to an end in the year of Capitan Chiquito's birth with the achievement of Mexican independence in 1821.[12]

The Apache people once dominated an area about the size of France and are now a sovereign nation about the size of Delaware. The combined population today of both the San Carlos and White Mountain Reservations is approximately 25,000. I have lived for over two decades on the San Carlos Apache reservation, and it is not difficult for me to imagine what accomplished warriors and horsemen the great-grandparents of these people were. When I attend their rodeos and observe their equestrian skills, I can envision their ancestors thundering across the desert plains in pursuit of cattle and horses. Numerous books, legends, and movies have been inspired by this fascinating culture. The Apache people are understandably somewhat reserved and mistrustful of newcomers to the reservation, but once you earn their trust they are friends forever. Some of the new nurses and physicians that came to the hospital I worked in would complain to me about the rudeness and ungratefulness of the Apache people for their help to them. I would remind them that the Apache people have given up much over the past 150 years, and that if they had visited here at that time it would be at the risk of their lives. Even after living in San Carlos for over twenty years and becoming a familiar person in the community, I would never walk the streets at night. I have seen hundreds of assaulted people in our emergency room that made the mistake of being out on foot after dusk. There are gangs of Apache boys who still have the warrior spirit in them and few outlets for entertainment. In the hot summer months, one form of entertainment is to throw matches in the brittle dry grasses. The tribe has appointed a member of their Forestry Department to take boys who have been found to be starting fires and teach them about nature and the benefits and beauty of the forest. A skateboarding arena and the Boys and Girls Club have also been introduced for healthy youth activities. The Apache still love to hunt elk, deer, and many other animals on the reservation.

Few Apache people visit Mexico these days, but when they do they are sometimes given trouble at the border crossing for appearing to be Mexican. There is much Mexican blood flowing in Apache veins, due to the numerous Mexican woman and children they captured. Likewise, many Apache children were captured in Mexico and raised as slaves. There was a time in the not too distant past when the Apaches were the terror of Sonora and Chihuahua and raided even farther south than that.

A Jesuit priest, Father Juan Nentvig, writes of the Apache raiding activities in his description of Sonora and Arizona in 1764:

> Even though they are scattered over a large area, one surmises their vast numbers by the many raids which occur simultaneously in this province. At the time they are plundering in Sonora there are war parties of two to three hundred in the Pimería Alta. And there are about the same number raising havoc in Janos, and still others bring ruin and desolation as far as the interior of Nueva Viscaya while others are active in Chihuahua. At the same time there are still Apaches in their many rancherias guarding their women and children. Therefore, it is not beyond the realm of possibility that their numbers exceed one thousand families. It is God's merciful design that the Apache scatter their forces over a large area and do not as a unit attack us, for there could be no place within the entire province that could be held against a united Apache effort. The whole province could be destroyed within a year. This is something to fear because the enemy is changing his tactics. Previously they attacked only two or three times a year, always at full moon. Now they attack at any time and in large numbers. They come in the dark when they are least expected, and the ranchers are negligent in keeping watch. Moreover, the marauders have no fear of our troops and in their retreat are able to reach a mountain stronghold where they have time to rest a stolen herd.[13]

The Apache had no desire to destroy or eliminate the Spanish provinces. They were harvesting the Spanish horses and cattle, just as they harvested their crops of corn when the time was right.

The grandson of Capitan Chiquito, Lonnie, would sometimes point to a small, lone, singular cloud in the sky and say, "That is an Apache cloud. The Apaches would travel in small bands, but when there was a crisis or a threat to their people, they would all come together and create a thunderstorm."

From Capitan Chiquito's own testimony, he was born in a canyon called Aravaipa about eighty miles north of Tucson.[14] Aravaipa is a Hispanicized form of a Sobaipuri Indian name meaning "small" (*ali*) and "water" (*waxia*).[15]

The Sobaipuri Indians had occupied this canyon for centuries. It is a beautiful and wondrous place: a small creek flows through awesome canyon walls. It is rich in plant life and the animals that the plants sustain. By the time of Capitan's birth the canyon had been in Apache hands for seventy years.

The Jesuit missionary, Father Eusebio Francisco Kino, reports of a visit he took there in 1697. The Sobaipuri Indians were a subgroup of the Pima/Papago. They had taken to Christianity and their villages in Aravaipa had become a buffer zone against the Apache advance. There were ten Sobaipuri villages along the Aravaipa Creek. Chief Humari was the main chief. When you visit the Aravaipa today, there are still Sobaipuri pottery sherds scattered on the mesa top where the villages were.

Bolton writes of Kino's visit:

> As the explorers marched northward they traveled cautiously with scouts ahead, for on the right was Apache land, and Coro was not sure of his reception by Humari's people. Messengers went forward to notify the villages that the great Black Robe was coming, and everywhere the Spaniards met a ceremonious welcome and generous hospitality. Kino and the officers were lodged in houses built by the natives especially for the occasion. As he entered the settlements they found roads cleared and arches and crosses erected. Kino, aided by Manje and Acuna, dispensed Christian instruction and baptized children. Bernal appointed native officers, gave them canes with fluttering ribbons, accepted homage in the name of the King, and harangued the villagers about loyalty, duty, and particularly about war on the Apaches.[16]

The following year in February, Kino's mission at Cocospora was attacked by Apaches. The Jesuit missionary there, Father Pedro Ruiz, and other defenders put up a good fight, but the Pueblo was sacked and burned. Father Ruiz lost everything, even his clothes, and fled into the interior.[17]

My wife, Velma, and I once took a tour of the Kino missions of northern Sonora and saw the ruins of Cocospora. Many of the Kino missions are still active, and to this day on certain feast days of the Blessed Virgin, the townspeople still enact a drama where the Apaches come and steal the statue of the Blessed Virgin, then the men of the town pursue them to rescue the Virgin and bring her back into the church triumphantly.

The American historian Donald Worcester relates the following about the buffer that the Sobaipuris tribe created to protect the Spanish from the Apaches:

> Of all the Piman tribes the Sobaipuris were the most noted as warriors, for their lands bordered those of the Aravaipa Apaches and the Chiricahuas, and they occasionally pursued raiders deep into the Chiricahua Mountains. A weak tribe would soon have been driven away or annihilated. Despite their courage and skill of fighters, however, the Sobaipuris could not hold out against Apache pressure indefinitely.[18]

But this bulwark against the Apache invasion was not to last. By 1750 because of continued intense raids by the Apache, the Spanish officials intentionally relocated the Sobaipuri Indians. Aravaipa Canyon was now an Apache stronghold and a staging area for their raids into Spanish territory. It was an ideal place to corral the herds of cattle and horses that they would take from Spanish hands.

It is not known, but likely, that Capitan Chiquito held a different name as a boy. "Capitan Chiquito" is a "nom de guerre" (a war name), a sobriquet that is taken on after certain accomplishments. Spanish accounts relate encounters with another El Capitan Chiquito, or El Chiquito before his birth. This man could possibly be his father or grandfather. The Apache received the right of band leader, or chief, either through paternal succession or by demonstrating their abilities in raiding and warfare.

In 1797 Spanish records write of El Capitan Chiquito resisting their efforts to bring Apaches into their mission "establishments of peace." They chased him as far north as Zuni and described him as timorous, superstitious, and a witch diviner (foretelling the future, however, was a qualification for a good Apache chief).

"El Chiquito often invoked the supernatural against his enemies and employed this power to influence other Apaches."[19] At this time the

Apaches may also have considered the Spanish to be timorous and superstitious with their bloody Jesus on the cross that they often found
in the Spanish ranch houses.

Four years before Capitan Chiquito's birth, another man (possibly his
father) was written of in Spanish accounts:

> In Arizpe, a town in Sonora, in 1817, being Governor D. Esteban Echega-
> ray happened in the case of having apprehended the celebrated Apache
> chief called Capitan Chiquito, with three other captives in the same
> campaign, with the intentions of inspiring trust in them. They were
> treated with the utmost consideration in such a way that they were
> there as detainees, while other small captains that had asked for peace
> would arrive to which the government, as always, had deferred. Despite
> this and the benefits given to these detainees, soon to be set free (it
> only consisted of peace arrangements already asked for). Capitan Chiq-
> uito and his fellows took advantage of a guard slip where they were. He
> killed the night guard with his own gun and three more soldiers, taking
> their weapons. The four Apaches escaped through the same town plaza
> of the capital yelling and screaming all the way.[20]

In the year of Capitan Chiquito's birth, Spain would surrender its
investment in Mexico. The Apache "problem" would now be a Mexican
problem. Mexico would develop a different policy toward the Apache.

3

The Apache War with Mexico

SOME MAY HAVE SEEN the soldiers coming and hid themselves from their view. Yet three Apache hunters did not see the large group of the enemy advancing, because they were very busy with hunting with a "fire-drive." The Apaches would sometimes set fires to clear land for farming, but they also used fire-drives to direct fleeing animals toward waiting hunters. Three men were involved in this hunting method when the smoke drew the attention of 154 Mexican soldiers on an expedition to find and kill Apaches. They were from the Mexican presidio at Tucson. When the soldiers spotted the three Apaches advancing toward them, their captain ordered them to hide in ambush. Two of the Apache hunters were ahead of the one who started the fires; when they drew close to the soldiers, one was killed and the other mortally wounded.

Chiquito was a boy of nine at this time. Perhaps he and his friends were busy trying to coax a desert rat out of its nest, as some Apache boys still do today. A few of the boys will poke sticks into the nest, while another boy waits at the only undisturbed hole with a large rock in his hand to crush the rat's back when it comes out of its lair. The desert rats usually live in tunnels under a large clump of cactus and are still considered good to eat by some. Among the boys there were possibly some Mexican captives that the Apaches raised as their own. All Apache children had been taught to become "invisible" when danger came. They were taught to pull their power inside themselves and be as silent and calm as the bottom of the lake and make themselves "one" with whatever rock, tree, or bush they decided to conceal themselves with.

Chiquito may have remembered this incident from his boyhood, as it took place near the mouth of Aravaipa Canyon where he lived and was born. One of the hunters returned to the Apache camp with his wounded comrade, who had been stabbed in the lung with a lance. He died soon afterward. When they saw the troop depart, some of the men ran to collect the body of their fallen friend. Later that night the wails of the two widows began that would make a haunting melody in chorus with the coyote howls and hoots of the owls.

Raids such as this one, led by the Mexican Captain Antonio Comaduran in May 1830, perhaps built a determination by Chiquito to one day be a leader who would protect and revenge his people.[1] Perhaps he was beginning to develop the visionary powers that a chief must have to foresee danger and that would keep his men from harm on raids into Mexico. Anthropologist William Griffen notes that "foretelling the future was a qualification necessary for a good Apache chief." Griffen also states: "Chiefs were chosen informally. Although it was easier for sons of a strong leader to be selected, the position was not hereditary. A man had to prove himself and be accepted by his fellows."[2]

Chiquito was trained like a Spartan since boyhood, as he was born in a time of war and danger to the Apache people. The Aravaipa band that Chiquito was born into was called the Tsejine (the people of the Dark Rocks). This name came from a mountain in the southernmost range of their territory where there were numerous darkly colored rocks. The mountain was Dzil Nazaayu (mountain that sits here and there: Bassett Peak). Aravaipa Creek was the hub of their territory, which extended about fifty miles in all directions around the creek. The rancherias in Aravaipa Canyon were their home base, and they had farm sites throughout the canyon and on many other creeks in their territory. They would often travel from their home base to hunt and gather wild foods, and they would leave their territory to conduct raids on the Mexican ranches and missions to the south.[3]

William Griffen writes as follows on the training of Apache boys:

> Apaches educated their youth to be good warriors and raiders so that
> they would be good providers as adults. Ideally, boys trained rigorously
> and practiced running long distances, mounting horses, shooting with
> the bow, parrying with the lance, jumping into cold water, and simi-
> lar activities to toughen themselves and perfect fighting skills. They
> learned about animals and studied their reactions, since animals often
> were aware of an approaching enemy sooner than were humans. Part
> of the adolescent training was the quest of the vision that would bring
> supernatural aid so that a boy could become a successful warrior. Divine
> assistance was especially valuable to a boy on his first four campaigns
> since they determined his future as a fighter.[4]

Chiquito may have longed for the day when he could be apprenticed
to a warrior and go on his first raid, but in the summer of 1832 he was
eleven years old and needed to wait three more years for this initiation.
Perhaps Chiquito especially admired a war chief of his band named Capitan Chiquito, whose name and power he would one day earn. There was a
group of Apache that had decided to live and farm under the protection
of the Mexican presidio at Tucson, but Capitan Chiquito had convinced
a group of these Apaches to join him and twenty-five of his warriors in
Aravaipa Canyon.

The priest at the mission at Cocospera had organized a meeting to
call for volunteers to form a militia and choose a military leader of the
group. Joaquin Vicente Elias was chosen to command the militia on an
expedition to attack the Apaches at Aravaipa Canyon.

Young Chiquito may have been watching and wishing he could join
the meeting of the war chief Capitan Chiquito with his twenty-five warriors and others who had abandoned the presidio at Tucson. Yet during
this gathering of Apache braves they were taken completely by surprise
by the militia of Mexicans. The Mexicans under Colonel Elias had somehow eluded their sentinels and crossed the creek from the south. There
were screams and war cries as the horses of this militia went from a trot
to a gallop straight toward the gathering of warriors. Chiquito may have
run to help the women and children find a safe place to hide, because
he was not taken captive. Many of the Apache men in the meeting were
shot or lanced in a short time, but then the soldiers went farther into
the canyon to kill more victims and to capture any children they could.
They opened the corral and stole over two hundred horses and mules.

The attack went on for four hours, and the Apaches could not rally themselves in large enough numbers in one place to take on this force of two hundred armed soldiers.

On June 27, 1832, the governor of Sonora wrote to the governor of Chihuahua about this victory:

> Your Excellency, since your jurisdiction of Chihuahua and ours of Sonora are both beleaguered by the cruel and indomitable Apaches, we feel we should share the good news of any advantage we gain over them. Besides, we have always treated one another as neighbors and brothers in the Republic we support together. In Aravaipa Canyon on the fourth day of the present month, a force of some two hundred of our citizen volunteers engaged our common enemy on their own ground. After a relentless and valiant attack that lasted all of four hours, our citizens proclaimed a complete victory. Seventy-one Apache warriors lay dead on the field. Thirteen under age captives were taken. Two hundred and sixteen horses and mules were recovered. God and liberty![5]

After this attack, the leader of the Mexican expedition returned all of the branded animals to their owners. He let the men who had captured children keep them. The rest of the animals were distributed among the men, except for three mules that he gave to the wife of Roque Somosa, the only Mexican killed in the attack. Twelve of his men were wounded. Not everyone was pleased with news of this victory, as many feared bloody Apache retaliation. The justice of the peace for the village of San Ignacio wrote to the governor, "Now we will have them in our homes!," and he implored him to send twenty-five muskets and ammunition.[6]

About 1835 when Chiquito was fourteen years old, it would have been determined that he was ready to go on his first raid into Mexico as an apprentice. For four days he would take lessons alone in a wickiup for half the day with an experienced warrior, who would tell him what was expected of him. For these four days he could not wash or touch water and he must sleep at night on a rock or mano. The war cap made for him was not like that of the experienced warrior with large eagle feathers but a novice warrior's cap with the feathers from four birds: the quail, the oriole, the downy feathers of the eagle, and two hummingbird wing pin feathers for speed. As he left the village for his first raid he would be anointed with pollen and everyone would wish that things would go well for him. For the first four days of the journey into Mexican territory he was not to look back home. He should keep his thoughts focused on the horses and cattle that they wished to obtain. At night he would sleep with his head on a rock to keep himself alert, always with his head to the east. There were certain words that must be used that were different from the regular words for a woman, a horse, water, the Mexican, and many others. If you did not use these words then things would not go right. He was to be a servant to the other warriors: cooking their food and gathering firewood and doing any other tasks they wanted him to do in obedience and without question. He was to drink only through a cane straw and not let water touch his lips. And he had a special scratch stick to touch his body with because he was not to scratch with his fingers. If the raid was successful he would bring these objects back to his mother, who would put them away for his next raid. If he was successful in his second raid, then his mother would keep them for another son.

After two successful raids, he was not considered a novice anymore, but he must still observe the taboos, use the warpath language, and follow the instructions of the war chief. As he became a more accomplished warrior, had good fortune on raids, and showed himself to be mindful and respectful of the older warriors, then they might share "words of power" for protection and skills useful in battle. A medicine man was believed to have "Star Power," and he could be consulted to obtain the use of power. There were various powers such as wind power, bat power, running power, and the power to foresee future events.[7]

In 1834 the Mexican presidio at Tucson learned of a planned attack on the towns of Tubac and Santa Cruz by the Apaches in large numbers. To counter this offensive the Mexican army sent five hundred soldiers north, penetrating Aravaipa and Pinal territory as far as the Salt River and on to the Mogollon Mountains. This was a great surprise to the Aravaipa and their sister band, the Pinals, as the Mexican army had never invaded their country so deeply. The Apaches had probably also received word from the Comanche and the Chiricahua to the east of them that the president of Mexico, Santa Anna, and six thousand of his troops had crossed the Texas border to crush the rebellion of the Texans. The Apache must have realized that the same could be done to them. To the surprise of the officials in Tucson, they were approached by representatives of the Aravaipa and Pinal bands to make a peace treaty. On the very day that Santa Anna and his troops were laying siege to a small mission in San Antonio called the Alamo, the following treaty was made with the Aravaipa and Pinal band on March 5, 1836:

(1) That they submit themselves to the government of the Mexican nation and promise to observe its laws.

(2) That, as a consequence, no Mexican troop will attack them, just as no troop has attacked them since they asked for peace.

(3) That they pledge themselves as allies of our troops against all aggressors, even if they were their own neighbors, the Tonto or the White Mountain nations.

(4) That they agree to return any female captives to us provided we returned two already captured Apaches to them, one captured by the Gila Pimas and the second a captive presently at Nacameri in central Sonora.

(5) That they promise not to make peace with other nations, the Janeros particularly, without previous consent of the Mexican government.

(6) That they agree not to harm any Mexican citizen.

(7) That no Apache travel farther south than Tucson without a passport from the Tucson commander, to be issued in no more than four or five Apaches at any one time.

(8) That for the time being they settle at the junction of the Aravaipa Arroyo and the San Pedro River, or later at another place with the approval of the Tucson commander. Obeying these conditions, they are to be provided with rations supplied to other peaceful Apaches and the tools and oxen necessary to cultivate the earth.

(9) That every two weeks they report to the Tucson commandant on occurrences in their region, particularly any advance signs of hostile attack.

(10) That the door remain open for the further peace treaties already requested by the Tonto and the White Mountain nations. To accomplish this, those nations must declare the number of warriors, women, and children in their bands and arrange with the Tucson commander for their place of settlement.[8]

However, conflict between the Apache and other non-Apache tribes, such as the Pima and Papago, continued. In the late summer of 1837, Chief Azul of the Gila River Pima brought the commandant of the Tucson presidio fifteen pairs of Apache ears, expecting to obtain the usual reward for evidence of enemy dead.[9]

The peace with Mexico did not last long. In the 1840s the population of Sonora decreased drastically due to Apache attacks on the Sonoran villages of Arizpe, Fronteras, and Tucson. Sonora took a drastic step by offering 100 pesos for the scalp of any Apache warrior of fourteen years or older. There were also bounties of fifty pesos for the scalps of women, and twenty-five pesos for those of children. Anglos from Texas were now coming into Arizona and taking advantage of the scalp trade. The Mexican province of Chihuahua was the next to offer bounties for the scalps of the Apache. By the end of 1849 Chihuahua City had become the "scalp capital of America." They had paid out enormous sums for Apache scalps, but the Apache still killed people on the outskirts of the city. There was no way to prove that the scalps that were brought in were those of Apaches. Many of them were those of Mexicans, Pimas, or other tribes.[10]

On a warm day in September 1847, Chiquito was most likely working in one of his fields of corn. At the age of twenty-seven he had not only become a renowned warrior, but he was also respected as an accomplished agriculturalist. He managed several crops of corn and fruit trees that he irrigated from the waters of Aravaipa Creek. He now had three wives, one of whom was a Mexican captive.

Perhaps he was working in the fields, teaching his son how to entice fruit and grain from the earth. The first sign of danger they heard may have been a bugle call, or the sound of drumming and the frightening pounding of horses in full gallop. He was not a boy anymore, expected to hide or to help the women and children to hide. He was one who had attained power in battle. He probably ran to his wickiup to claim his weapons of bow and arrow, and to help to rally the men. But they were considerably outnumbered by two hundred mounted Mexican soldiers. His fellow warriors put up a brave defensive, yet the Mexican troops killed sixteen of his warriors and also killed four boys and seven women. They took fourteen prisoners, probably women and children. They also took thirty horses and eight head of cattle, which the Apache had previously taken from them. This attack on Aravaipa Apaches was led by Captain Comaduran who had led previous expeditions to Aravaipa Canyon. He had warned the Aravaipa Apache that if they did not cease to attack Tubac and San Xavier and surrender all the families in the canyon that they would be punished.[11]

From the ages of sixteen to twenty-six Capitan Chiquito distinguished himself in battle and demonstrated his power and ability to plan an enemy attack. By 1848 he, no doubt, had demonstrated his abilities as a leader and earned the "nom de guerre" (war name) of his predecessor, Capitan Chiquito. Capitan Chiquito literally means "the little Captain." This did not necessarily refer to his stature, because the Spanish often referred to the war chiefs as Capitancilla. Yet Chiquito was short in stature. His height is reported as five feet, three-fourths inches.[12] As a war chief he had demonstrated his abilities to plan a strategy of attack. And he was known to possess "power against enemies." He could use this power to give his men protection and good luck. On the warpath the chief never hauled wood or water and never did camp work. He kept quiet, unless he was instructing his men on how they should perform the attack and counsel them on dangers, such as snakes, mountain lions, and scorpions. He was considered a man equal to twelve men. Yet when they were not on the warpath and back in their rancherias, he was a common man. When he went out hunting deer, or worked in the fields on their crops, he was not in charge. He was like any other man. It was only on the warpath that his word was sacrosanct. The leader of the Aravaipa band at this time was a man named Hashke Bahnzin (called Eskiminzin by the whites). Capitan Chiquito was usually referred to as his subchief or war chief. On the warpath they would always bring a medicine man along to heal the men of any injuries or sickness. The medicine man of the Aravaipa band was a chief called Santo.[13]

I wonder if the visionary powers of Capitan Chiquito had forewarned him of a new threat that would soon challenge the safety of his homeland.

CHAPTER

4

A New Invasion

The Coming of the Americans

PERHAPS CAPITAN CHIQUITO HAD the same intuitive "star power" that the Spanish had noted in his ancestor. My wife, Velma, had mystical experiences that she called "visitations." She usually had these while lying on her bed resting and would go into a kind of euphoric trance. She could speak, but she could not move her body. I can visualize Chiquito on a cold December night in 1848 going into the kind of otherworldly trance that I sometimes witnessed Velma do. I can imagine him sharing his vision with the medicine man, Santo, the following day in the beautiful tonal Apache language:

> In my vision I saw them. They were men with white faces, riding on horses with fierce determination from the east. They had hair on their faces and smelled like sour milk. They had no warpaint, yet their bodies were covered in the blue of the sky. They carried a symbol of their power on a wooden pole before them. It was of three colors and it flapped in the wind. Their flag was covered with white stars, like the ones I had seen fall from the sky in my boyhood.

Santo and Capitan Chiquito may have wondered if these men, or some of these men, had "star power" like the flag they carried. The Apache at this time almost completely dominated the northern frontier of Mexico

32

and took what they needed to survive. Yet both chiefs would pray to Usen now to protect their people from this new force that threatened their safety and way of life.

The commander of the northern frontier presidios, Don Ignacio Zuniga, estimated that from 1820 to 1835 there had been five thousand Mexicans killed, one hundred settlements destroyed, and about four thousand settlers forced to leave the region. Most of the rancherias of northern Sonora had been left in ruins, except for the garrisoned towns of Tucson and Tubac. Even the important town of Fronteras was in the hands of the Apaches by 1848.[1]

The Texans had won their revolution against Mexico. The president of Mexico, Santa Anna, had been captured by the Texans and many wanted him hung. Yet the new president of the Republic of Texas, Sam Houston, kept him prisoner in Texas until they had worked out a treaty of independence; he then allowed Santa Anna to return to Mexico. There was great animosity between Mexico and the United States when Texas was annexed into the Union in 1845. Subsequent border clashes resulted in a declaration of war on Mexico by the United States.

At the end of the Mexican-American war the Treaty of Guadalupe Hidalgo of 1848 gave the United States New Mexico, the Arizona land below the Gila River, and California for the sum of $15 million. The territory of the Aravaipa Apache and the town of Tucson were not acquired by the United States until the 1854 Gadsden purchase, when the United States gave Mexico $10 million for this land that they wanted for a transcontinental railroad.

Apache relations with the newly arriving Anglo-Americans began in a relatively friendly manner. Various Apache bands had been in contact with traders, trappers, and bounty hunters for at least twenty years, and they offered friendship to early military officers who crossed through their region. Yet by the early 1850s the seeds for further troubles were sown. Historian Oakah L. Jones Jr. writes:

> The Apaches could not accept the United States insistence that raids
> into Mexico must stop. They could not understand why the Anglos
> thought they owned the land by treaty with Mexico when the Mexicans
> had never really conquered Apacheria. They were willing, however, to
> allow the Anglos to pass through their domain and to permit settlement
> there on a regulated basis if settlers would pay them for the privilege.

However they would not accept the concept of widespread and unregulated settlement into their region, and this led to the first confrontations, with miners who moved in the Santa Rita del Cobre area of southwestern New Mexico in the mid-1850s.[2]

I have had a number of confrontations with Apache men on the reservation also, especially in the emergency room where emotions and tensions are often high. I learned to focus and be calm. It could be very intimidating to have a large, protective father looking over your shoulder as you tried to place an intravenous needle in the arm of his child. You wanted to do it right the first time.

One night as I was watching television on the weekend with Velma, a shirtless Apache man appeared at our house trying to open the sliding glass door to our living room. I went and got my 37 magnum S&W revolver and told him to get out of our house. When I saw that he was intoxicated and confused, I took him by the arm and led him outside to sit in a lawn chair on the porch. I prepared to call the tribal police and told him to wait there. All of a sudden, he jumped over our porch railing and began to throw rocks at me and call me names. I was told that the police found him later by the San Carlos River full of cactus thorns. I met this young man several times later in the emergency room, and we became friends. He told me that he was confused that night and thought he was entering his own home.

The historian Donald Worcester writes: "If, in fact, the Aravaipa actually carried out the devastating raids credited to them, they were, man for man, the most destructive band in Arizona. One Apache band alone had stolen an estimated one hundred thousand horses."[3]

It is difficult sometimes for me to imagine the drastic and culturally devastating changes that the Apaches have experienced over the last 150 years. I get a sense sometimes of their ancestral soul when I hear their chants and the whirlwind sound of the bull roarer, as I sit on my porch in the evening and listen to the Sunrise Dance.

The Sunrise Dance is a three-day ritual performed for an Apache girl as she comes into womanhood. She is given power and blessings for a long life from "Changing Woman" (a sacred female being). She actually "becomes one" with Changing Woman and imparts her blessings to the people. She has a cattail pollen liquid poured over her head by the medicine man as a catalyst for her transformation. As she is in this divine state, she blesses the people gathered with cattail pollen and the energy that has infused it. At the ritual are four *gaan* dancers (mountain spirits) and one vortex leader with a bull roarer. The bull roarer is a piece of wood from a tree that has been struck by lightning. It is on a string and is whirled about to create a whirlwind sound. It is part of the ritual to pull down power from the Creator. The four *gaan* dancers (to the best I can understand in my Christian symbolism) are like the four Archangels. They each have symbols on their headdresses representing the four directions. At one point in the dance, the people line up to have the *gaan* dancers bless them with the laying on of hands.

An Apache girl must have much stamina to complete the ordeal of the Sunrise Dance, as for three days she is almost constantly dancing or running in place. I attended the Sunrise Dance of Lorena Cosen, who is the daughter of my Apache godchild, Melissa. At Lorena's dance her cousin, Shanaya Victor, was her partner and helped guide her through the ceremony. Lorena in turn was the partner for Shanaya's sister, Janessa, during her dance.

It seems to me that the Sunrise Dance is somewhat of an initiation or blessing for Apache boys also. The identity of the masked *gaan* dancers is a mystery to me. When these boys or men allow themselves to take on this spiritual role, they are vessels of what I would call "angelic power." The Sunrise Dance is really a rejuvenation of the spirit for the whole community.

Perhaps hunting for their first deer or elk has taken the place of their first war party raid for some. Those who do hunt often have similar taboos and rituals as the raids of old into Mexico.

An old wagon master speaking to a cavalry officer had this to say about the Aravaipa Apache: "We have a horror of them that you feel for a ghost. We never see them, but when on the road are always looking over our shoulders in anticipation. When they strike, all we see is the flash of the rifle resting with secure aim over a pile of stones, behind which, like a snake, the red murderer lies at full length."[4] I am sure that the Apaches also had some demeaning descriptions of the "white murderers" who sought to hunt and kill their tribal members.

As a member of our hospital's health education committee, I once organized a hike to the top of Mount Triplet, a prominent mountain peak on the reservation. I called it the "Mount Triplet Health Expedition," and I gave a promotional talk at the San Carlos high school to invite any interested boy or girl on the hike. Jeanette Cassa, a medicine woman and the granddaughter of Apache Chief Juh, also talked to the students about the importance of Mount Triplet in Apache culture. On the morning of the hike about twenty students showed up. We had a flag commemorating the hike that we would place at the summit. The students who participated in the expedition were perhaps on the high school track team or involved in sports, because, although my hobby was climbing the many mountains on the reservation, half of the students were at the top of the mountain before I had hardly hiked halfway.

The Indian fighting General Wesley Merritt spoke thus of the stamina of the Apache:

> All the Apaches are foot men, and mountain climbers. They will steal horses and use them, but when driven into the mountains the horses become a part of their rations. Graceful, well formed, with legs of steel wire, light and active as a cat, the Apache on the rocky hillside is unapproachable, and to fight him with any chances of success, he has to be attacked with skill and great caution at gray dawn in his bivouac far up among the rocks.[5]

When we see photos of the Apache in this time period, they are sleek and strong and full of energy. The Apache today struggle with the results of their conquest. McDonald's, Burger King, and the "Apache Burger" on the main highway through the reservation have not assisted them in regard to their health. Some medical researchers theorize that the Apache have a "feast and famine" gene. Because of the long periods where food was scarce, the Apache body learned to store energy in fat deposits in their system. Now that food is available at all times, some struggle with obesity and diabetes.

Dr. Ralph Ogle writes of the Apaches' increasing dominance of Arizona Territory and northern Mexico:

> The Apaches became so aggressive in early 1852 that they practically held the country to the east and west of the Rio Grande Valley. Not only this, but also in their raids (which the United States had pledged herself to stop) they were practically driving civilization from northern Mexico. In that part of Mexico, which was soon to be known as the Gadsden Purchase, travelers and adventurers found the region a land of widows, in which all agricultural activity had stopped, and where in the eastern part, even pastoral activities were carried on under the protection of field pieces. In the western part Tucson and Tubac with a combined population of 1,009, [the Apache] maintained a most precarious hold.[6]

The United States decided to create four permanent posts to stop the raids until the Apaches were forced to give up their predatory habits. One of these posts, called Camp Aravaypa, was established at the confluence of Aravaipa Creek with the San Pedro River. Yet after the outbreak of the US Civil War the army post was abandoned and burned in 1862. As the majority of military protection was withdrawn from Arizona during the Civil War, the number and boldness of Apache raids increased.

It was about this time that Capitan Chiquito captured a young Mohave girl on a raid on a Mohave village near present-day Phoenix. This young girl would eventually become one of his wives and the one that would remain with him throughout his life.[7]

A Mexican American man, who was to become Capitan Chiquito's nemesis, was a Tucson rancher and Indian fighter named Jesus Maria Elias. Jesus and his brother, Juan, had been born and raised in the Tucson area and had become citizens of the United States after the Gadsden Purchase. They were highly regarded ranchers and citizens of the community, respected by the Papago, Mexicans, and Anglos alike. They were very involved in local and territorial government. Jesus stated that the Apache had been fighting his father, robbing his cattle, and killing his people ever since he could remember. His brother Juan said that his first recollection was the day that he learned that a large band of Apaches had ambushed twenty soldiers and citizens from Tucson on some nearby mountain, killing all of the Tucsonans after they ran out of ammunition. In 1850 and again in 1851, Juan would witness such conflicts firsthand when the Apache attacked Tucson itself, slaying several of its residents and driving away much of its livestock. In 1853, Apache violence would again touch Juan and Jesus's family: the boys' uncle, Jose M. Orosco, was slain while attempting to defend a ranch in Calabasas from a raid led by what those in Tucson insisted was a combined party of Apaches and Americanos.[8]

The Elias brothers had suffered much from raids by the Aravaipa band and other Apache bands. In these raids two of their brothers, Ramon and Cornelio, had lost their lives. In November 1861 Juan's brother, Ramon, was killed while on an expedition to recapture some cattle. The livestock recovery attempts were made after requests for help from the US government went unheeded. It fell to Juan and Jesus to recover their brother's corpse. When they finally located Ramon's remains in the

Tortolita (Turtle Dove) Mountains north of Tucson, they discovered that the Apaches had crushed Ramon's hands with rocks, which the brothers interpreted as "a sign that he was a brave enemy." According to Juan's great-grandson, Ramon Elias (no doubt a namesake of his ancestor), Ramon's wife, Ignacia, was also killed and scalped by Apaches in this raid.[9] On this raid it was reported that there were two hundred to three hundred Apaches, part of them from Cochise's and Capitan Chiquito's bands, that raided the Elias Ranch and took seventy-five cattle and twenty-five horses. On these raids Jesus Elias stated that the Apache "always hollered and shouted that they were brave and could lick Frenchman, Americans, Mexicans, and everybody!"[10]

Juan Elias's great-grandson, Ramon, related to me that his great-grandfather had two daughters, Gertrudis and Juanita. His great aunt, Tia Juanita, would visit his family when he was a young boy and stay in the room where he slept. Ramon told me this story:

At night before falling asleep my Tia would often tease me and tell stories. Many of the stories were about her encounters with "El Cucuy" [author's note: El Cucuy is a mythical ghost-monster—a Mexican version of the bogeyman]. She said to beware when the moon is full because this is when the Cucuy comes out to cause terror and mischief. She said, "El Cucuy era un mal asesino sinvergüenza Apache." In other words, he was an evil murderous Apache scoundrel. He lurked about during full moon nights stealing anything he could including innocent young girls! She repeatedly described how she saw El Cucuy stalk the Rancho where she and sister Tula lived. She described the experience as terrifying and frightening. Her family would gather on full moon nights and sleep close together for protection and safety "por si acaso," just in case. Her father and brothers would take turns "a la vigilancia," being watchful. Tia Juanita slept in my room sitting in a chair by the window on full moon nights. She seemed visibly restless. Her stories were scary and thrilling. She always said she wanted me to grow up brave and strong to protect her, Tia Tula, and my sisters from "El Cucuy." At the time I tended to think she was messing with me. It became apparent as I became more familiar with our family history in my adult years, that Tia Juanita's stories were actual experiences she had while living on the Elias Ranch near the San Xavier mission in the 1880s! One attack on the Juan Elias Ranch was documented to have taken place in April of 1883. I estimate Tia Tula was about 5 years old and Tia Juanita was an infant at the time.[11]

In April 1863, a large group of Aravaipa, Pinal, and Chiricahua Apache attacked Saint Xavier and took one hundred head of steer belonging to Juan Elias. While pursuing this group of Apache, they caught up with the rearguard of six Indians and had a skirmish in which Cornelio Elias was shot mortally in the head. In a follow-up scouting party attempting to recover the cattle, they found about forty of them in Aravaipa Canyon. They ate some of the cattle, distributed some of them to the men who had volunteered, and returned about twenty of them to Juan Elias.[12]

In 1863 to avenge the deaths of his two brothers and his uncle, Jesus María Elias led an attack on the Apaches of Aravaipa Canyon. This group was made up of civilians from Tucson, Papago Indians from San Xavier, and a group of twenty-five union soldiers from California on their way east to fight the Confederates.[13]

One morning as the Apache slept in their wikiups, they were awakened with terror at the sound of a bugle and Papago war cries. They saw white men in blue uniforms, and they were carrying their flag of stars on a pole in front of them. As they entered the Apache village and began to shoot and club them and burn the wickiups, the Apache gathered their women and children and ran to the high grounds where the horses could not follow. When the gunshots stopped and the horses galloped away, they returned to the smoky remains of their village. There were screams and cries of anguish from men and women both, as they beheld fifty of their people dead on the ground. It would take days for them to bury the dead with the proper ceremonies. They knew the man who led this attack, and they vowed that they would kill him. He was named after the God of the Mexicans and the white man. His name was Jesus.

Two years later the white men in blue returned and rebuilt their fort where the waters of the Aravaipa flow into the San Pedro. The Apache had to move their villages to the south near the mountain called Nadahcho sian (Mescal Mountain). The soldiers named their fort after the hero of the war where the Americans were trying to kill each other. His name was Grant.

One day on a visit to Washington, DC, Capitan Chiquito would meet the fort's namesake: President Ulysses S. Grant.

5

The Apache War against the Americans

BY 1867 JESUS ELIAS was hired by the US Army as a guide for Camp Grant. He had a farm three miles north of the fort along the San Pedro River in an area that was now considered relatively safe from attack due to military protection. The Apache bands led by Chief Eskiminzin of the Pinal Mountains and Capitan Chiquito of the Sierra Mescal had not forgotten the expedition that Jesus had led into their canyon and the lives that he took. They watched his comings and goings and were aware that he slept outside his house on a wooden cot during the warm summer months. With a shotgun in his hand that was packed with mescal seeds, an Apache assassin came out of the darkness and with a loud blast filled him full of pellets in his upper shoulder and lower neck.

Returning to their camp with the good news that Jesus had been killed, the Aravaipa band had a great feast and dance in celebration of the event. Yet they were later to learn that it was not Jesus who had been shot, but his brother, Juan, and to their further disappointment, Juan had survived his wounds. While Juan was recovering in the Camp Grant infirmary, the Aravaipa band again attacked the Elias farm, as Jesus was cutting brush in the fields. He had seen them coming and as he hid in the bushes he recognized them as rivals from the bands of Eskiminzin and Capitan Chiquito. The Apache took five horses and five cattle and killed two men who worked for Jesus.[1]

John Terrell writes of the sentiments of people in the East toward the government's efforts to conquer the Apache:

> Religious, fraternal, civic, service, and even some strong political organizations in the East and Middle West vociferously opposed warfare against the Apache and other Southwestern Indians. The residents of Arizona and New Mexico were excoriated for their wantonness, greed, and brutality. The Army was condemned for failing to protect the helpless Indians from these murderous civilians. The popularity of these views steadily increased, and the politicians began to listen.[2]

Yet the people of the east were not having their homes and ranches raided, their loved ones killed, nor were they being subjected to the acts of terror the Apache employed. A paper read to the Arizona Pioneers Historical Society had this to say:

> Eskiminzin in his early days was indeed the terror of Tucson. His reputation for cruelty rested on something more substantial than just being the scapegoat for Cochise's depredations. Evidence of Eskiminzin's early life reveals that before giving up to the authorities at old Camp Grant, and making a vow to keep the peace, Eskiminzin had been no better than the general run of hostiles. As an illustration of his viciousness Goodwin [H. F. Goodwin, former governor of Arizona] tells of the attack in September, 1867, on two sutlers of old Camp Grant who were en route to their farm. One of them was found tied to his wagon wheel, head down over a fire, feet completely burned off, his body viciously tortured. Goodwin tells too, of two killings by Eskiminzin on the San Pedro River near Tres Alamos in the same year. Several men bringing hay to the army post only three miles from Camp Grant. The following year Eskiminzin fell upon an army ambulance containing a major and a number of soldiers and killed almost all of them. Nelson A. Miles recorded one refined piece of torture characteristic of the Apaches that has been attributed to Eskiminzin. He was said to have buried a captive white man to the neck near a giant ant hill. The captive's mouth and eyes were coated with honey to attract the ants to their gruesome task. The victim survived two days while the ants ate the flesh from his skull.[3]

The viciousness and cruelty of the Apache toward their enemies must be understood in the context of their struggle: they were fighting invaders of their homeland and wanted to leave a clear message that this was their land! A popular T-shirt sold on the San Carlos reservation today shows Geronimo with three armed warriors and the caption: "Fighting Terrorists since 1492." The Apaches love holidays, but one holiday that they do not celebrate is Columbus Day.

The Apaches have a wonderful, but subtle, sense of humor. You can see this humor in some of the names of the communities on their reservation. Communities have names like "Ready-to-Go" (near a cemetery), "Home Alone" (where parents work or party and their children stay at home), "Moon-Base" (a community with a lunar landscape), "Jurassic Park" (a community near the river where you can imagine a Tyrannosaurus Rex appearing), and "The Darkest Corner" (a place of drug trafficking).

Terrell reports as follows on the ineffective military strategy in dominating the Apaches:

> The defensive strength of the entire Southwest suffered a severe setback by the transfer of Arizona Territory in January (1865) to the Department of California from the Department of New Mexico. Thus, Apacheria was divided between two commands, neither one of which could cooperate voluntarily with the other without specific orders from headquarters. Sometimes as long as three months would elapse before dispatches could be exchanged and the plans for an offensive could be coordinated and executed. The territorial government and the citizens were infuriated, but there was little they could do about the situation, except take matters into their own hands and defend themselves as best as they could.[4]

While higher officials were vacillating between a policy of complete extermination or reservation, many army officers were regularly doing "search and destroy" missions into Apache territory, killing any Apache they found and destroying all their resources.

In February of 1869, Colonel Reuben Bernard, a seasoned veteran of the Civil War, left Camp Grant on a "search and destroy" mission deep into Aravaipa Canyon, where he encountered Capitan Chiquito and his band. The soldiers were trudging through snow fifteen to twenty inches deep when they saw smoke on the mountainside and spotted forty Apaches fleeing up the mountain; the soldiers ordered a charge.

Colonel Bernard writes:

> Every man did his best to reach the fleeing Indians, but cavalry mounted as my company is, upon poor mustangs and broken down

stage horses, can do little in pursuing Indians up a snow-covered mountain. We continued up the mountain where we ran into another rancheria; here eight Indians were killed and six prisoners (women and children) were captured. The Indians lost all their camp equipment. The only things of any value captured were three bows and arrows, a few buckskins, butcher knives, awls, and a few baskets. Yet their captain, Chiquito, did not want peace.[5]

The commander of the Department of California was General E. O. C. Ord. Terrell writes of the many vacillating opinions on how to deal with the Apaches:

General Ord, faced with the realities of the situation, sent orders to General George Stoneman, in command in Arizona, to hunt down Apache as wild animals. Officers who killed the greatest number would be the first to receive promotion. Shortly afterward Ord changed his mind, and expressed the opinion that perhaps a reservation system was preferable to wholesale murder. The people of Arizona Territory didn't agree with him, and let him know it.

Captain John Barry, scouting in the White Mountains with sixty men, came upon a large number of Apache who displayed no signs of hostility. Around their villages were extensive fields of growing corn. Barry carried orders to kill any Apaches he confronted and destroy their resources. He disobeyed his orders and left in peace. His commander, Col. John Green, charged him with disobedience, but higher officers exonerated him.[6]

Colonel Bernard returned to Camp Grant on February 9, 1869, having marched 250 miles. On March 1 he set out again on another "search and destroy" mission, yet this time he had at his side an experienced guide and interpreter, Merejildo Grijalva. Grijalva had been captured from his Sonoran home as a boy by Cochise's band. He escaped from the Chiricahua in his early twenties. He spoke the Apache language well and knew their land and ways and customs. He was an invaluable guide to the American officers now, and he had no aversion to taking Apache scalps that some Arizona merchants still offered a bounty for.[7]

On March 19, Bernard's company descended into a deep canyon north of Mount Triplet on the San Carlos River. I have hiked into this canyon many times. You walk across a grassy plain, never suspecting the magnificent canyon before you until you are practically at its edge. Then you must find a path for descent, as the canyon walls are a shear drop-off. The few pathways into the canyon are marked by petroglyphs left by the ancient ones. At the canyon bottom you can find their cave dwellings and artifacts near pools of clear water and hidden waterfalls.

Bernard's company found a camp of nine huts and destroyed them. They captured two Apache women, one who was hiding in a pool of water, her body completely covered except for her nose. They forced the woman to lead them to another Apache camp of fifty-nine huts. Yet the huts were located strategically deep in the canyon bottom, and Bernard's company was spotted by the Apaches, who had ample time to flee; when the charge was ordered it took an hour for the soldiers to descend into the canyon bottom. They were shooting their guns at long range, so there were few Apaches killed. The soldiers destroyed "at least one ton of mescal, many bushels of roots, greens, nuts and other edibles, axes, hatchets, hoes, kettles, knives, bows and arrows, canteens, skins, manta blankets, paints, medicines, charms and needles."[8]

Travelers today on Highway 77 between Tucson and Winkelman will find the terrain has not changed a great deal since Lieutenant John Bourke described it in 1869. The beautiful rolling hills and canyons of the semiarid desert are still covered with majestic saguaro cactus in various anthropomorphic poses. The rocky hillsides hold an array of paloverde, cottonwood, and mesquite trees. The landscape holds a multitude of cacti, such as cholla, prickly pear, and the barrel cactus. The agave plant that grows in the canyon was one of the staple foods of the Apache, and they would roast it for several days in a pit.

Today you will find an occasional cross that notes a fatal car accident. Yet in Lieutenant Bourke's day, Bourke notes:

> On this march the curious rider could see much to be remembered all the days of his life. Piles of loose stones heaped up by loving hands proclaimed where the Apaches had murdered their white enemies. The projection of a rude cross of mescal or Spanish bayonet stalks was evidence that the victim was a Mexican, and a son of Holy Mother Church. Its absence was no index of religious belief, but simply of the nationality being American.[9]

On May 11, 1869, near the present town of Oracle on Highway 77, the Aravaipa Apaches made one of their most successful raids against the Anglo-American pioneers. This raid was no doubt led by Chief Ezkiminzin and Capitan Chiquito. Just one month previously troops from Camp Grant destroyed the rancheria, food, and belongings of two hundred Apaches in Aravaipa Canyon, leaving them starving and desperate. The previous day nine wagons and eighty mules owned by the Tully and Ochoa Company had left Tucson to bring supplies to Camp Grant on Aravaipa Creek. The fourteen teamsters with the wagon train were skilled Indian fighters. The caravan was led by wagon master Santa Cruz Castanida, who rode freely among the wagons mounted on a mule. The details of this battle became well known, because a miner and draftsman by the name of Edward Zinn had hitched a ride north on the wagon train. Zinn later painted in remarkable detail the various stages of the engagement in a 28-by-54-inch panel.

Edward Zinn's heart must have dropped to his feet when, about twenty-seven miles north of Tucson, the wagon train halted at the sight of over eighty Aravaipa Apaches blocking the road. The Apache interpreter called out to the wagon master: "Castanida, leave the wagons and you can go." The Apache-Spanish interpreter was Cisco, a Mexican man who was captured by the Apaches as a boy. Castanida had brought along a cannon loaded with grapeshot in one of his wagons, and he answered back: "You can have the wagons when we can no longer hold them." The Apaches had chosen their ambush site well, as there was no room for the wagons to form a circle with the canyon to one side and the hills on the other.

The Zinn painting shows that the attack begins at 8 a.m. with a fierce war cry from the Apaches. Zinn painted the Apache warriors in authentic detail wearing buckskin caps with turkey feathers and body paint of red and black dots. The Apache warriors are almost naked with muslin loincloths and pointed toe moccasins. Some have capes and red headbands and quivers full of arrows on their backs. The painting illustrates that the cannon begins to fire volley after volley of grapeshot at the surprised Apache. The Apaches have some rifles, but are mostly armed with bows and arrows. The painting even shows some Apaches using slings. When the cannon runs out of ammunition, the battle goes on until sunset with the teamsters firing rifles and pistols.

As the day progressed, a large band of Pinal warriors joined the Apache, and seven cavalrymen came to the aide of the teamsters. Zinn's painting shows the Apaches burning a captured teamster and the teamsters burying two of their fallen comrades. After a battle of ten hours, the cavalry leader, Sergeant Allison, decided it was time to retreat and leave the wagons and mules behind. The eleven surviving teamsters (two of them wounded), Zinn, and the seven cavalrymen (three of them wounded), began their march back to Tucson. The Apaches looted the wagons and captured all eighty mules, which would be used for food to fight another day.[10]

In July of 1869, out of Camp Goodwin farther to the north, Colonel John Green was scouring the countryside, killing Apaches and burning their crops wherever found. He went north along the San Carlos River tributaries burning acres and acres of corn. Then he went farther north to the White River in the White Mountains and found fields of corn that amazed him.

Colonel Green writes:

Soon after Captain Barry left I broke up camp and moved up White Mountain River about five miles to where I supposed was the central point of the cornfields and went into camp, then detailed all the men, except the small guard for camp, and commenced to destroy the corn. At least one hundred acres of fine corn, just in silk, were destroyed, and it took the command nearly three days to do it. I was astonished and could hardly believe that the Apache Indians could and would cultivate the soil to such an extent; and when we consider their very crude implements and the great labor it requires to dig the ditches for irrigation, one cannot help but wonder at their success. These fields compare very favorably with those of their more civilized brethren.[11]

Colonel Green is referring to his culture as "civilized" after he has destroyed over one hundred acres of much needed Apache corn. His civilized culture has just finished fighting each other for four years at the cost of over 800,000 American lives.

General Ord instructed Colonel John Green to find a suitable reservation in a place completely isolated from the whites. Here the Apache would be given provisions and forced to pursue agriculture. The wilder bands that resisted the solution would be exterminated. Colonel Green first built a road into the center of the White Mountain region where he established the post called Camp Ord, later called Fort Apache, at the road's terminus. The Apache, "because of their half starved condition, were eager to cooperate, and more than one thousand of them were present on July 1 for the first count and beef issue. By winter two thousand were under control, industriously cutting hay and wood which were purchased to the cooperation of General Stoneman."[12]

Another renowned Indian fighter of this period was Lieutenant Howard Bass Cushing. One of the officers that served with him stated that

Cushing "had killed more savages of the Apache tribe than any other officer or troop in the United States Army had done before or since."[13] It is a common practice in war to dehumanize the enemy by calling them "savages." In the Vietnam War, American soldiers called the Vietnamese combatants "gooks" or other demeaning names.

In December 1870 Lieutenant Cushing and his troops set out from Camp Grant marching north to the Mount Turnbull area, where they attacked a rancheria, destroying their property and scattering the Apaches to the hills. They burned all their winter stores, which was considered second only to the actual killing of Apaches in effectiveness. His troops scouted a great area from Camp McDowell, near present-day Phoenix, then traveled farther to the south to the Apache Mountains, where they laid waste to another rancheria, killing as many Apaches as they could and destroying their whole stock of supplies. He arrived in Tucson after this destructive mission on April 17, 1871.[14]

Lieutenant Cushing was not aware of this, but he was a marked man by the Apache and had about two weeks to live.

6

The Second Coming of Jesus (Elias)

ONE SPRING DAY IN 1994 Capitan Chiquito's grandson, Lonnie, took his daughter, Velma, and me to Aravaipa Canyon to show us the land that he had inherited from his grandfather. He pointed to the hill where his grandfather had lived and is now buried. He told us how white men had desecrated his grandfather's grave in their search for artifacts. He pointed to the place where a huge sycamore tree used to stand, and this is why the Apaches called this place Big Sycamore Stands Alone / Gashdla'a Choh O aa. He told us the story of how his father had once given him a horse and they traveled for two days from Old San Carlos to this place to meet his grandfather. They traveled through Hawk Canyon between Stanley Butte and Rawhide Mountain. They camped one night by a spring and continued to Aravaipa Canyon the next day. He remembered that as they approached the canyon they saw the awesome rock column called White Lady Sitting There. He said that his horse ate too much green spring grass, and it's belly swelled so greatly that the men had to poke a hole in its stomach with a sharp stick, hoping to expel the contents. However, the horse died and Lonnie said he cried like a baby.

Although Lonnie was aware of the massacre that had taken place here, he told us nothing about it. Traditionally, Apaches did not commemorate the dead, speak of the dead, or talk about bad things that have happened. I learned later about the massacre that had taken place here from three books on Lonnie's shelf: Elliott Arnold's *The Camp Grant Massacre*, Diana Hadley's *Environmental Change in Aravaipa*, and Don Schellie's *Vast Domain of Blood*. There were many sorrows that Lonnie kept in his heart and did not share, but I would sometimes see him weeping on his couch about some vision from the past that still troubled him. He once shared the story of how his father sent him and his sister, Audrey, off to boarding school. As they left Old San Carlos in a wagon they repeated over and over: "We will never forget the Apache. We will never forget the Apache. We will never forget the Apache."

The many army campaigns against the Apaches in recent years had made the bands of the Aravaipa and the Pinal desperate for food and water. The army's relentless stalking of them made farming and gathering an impossible task. They had been routed from their usual residences, and all of their stores of corn and mescal were destroyed. Reduced to the point of starvation, they reluctantly decided to make overtures of peace to the soldiers at Camp Grant.[1]

The commanding officer at Camp Grant at this time was First Lieutenant Royal Whitman of the Third US Cavalry. Notes from Lieutenant Whitman's journal state that on February 20, 1871, these Apache bands sent a group of five elderly women into Camp Grant under a flag of truce. They were fed and treated kindly for two days, and at their departure they told Whitman that a young chief would like to come in with a party to have a talk. Whitman encouraged the women to tell the chief to come and talk; Whitman wrote that a few days later a group of twenty-five Apaches rode cautiously into Camp Grant.[2] Terrell writes in his *Apache Chronicle*: "In the band were three well-known and dangerous Apache leaders, Eskiminzin (called Skimmy by the soldiers), Chiquito, and Santo."[3]

Eskiminzin told Lieutenant Whitman that he was chief of what was left of the Aravaipa Apache, which now numbered about 150. He said that he and his people were constantly being attacked by the cavalry and could get no rest. He said that the country along Aravaipa Creek from the San Pedro to the Galiuro Mountains had always been their home. Now they wanted to plant crops along the creek, be issued tools for that purpose, and be given rations until the crops came in. Whitman advised him to go north to Camp Apache in the White Mountains where Colonel Green had established a reservation for this purpose.

Eskiminzin explained: "That is not our country, neither are they our people. Our fathers and their fathers before them have lived in these mountains and have raised corn in this valley. We are taught to make mescal our principal article of food, and in the summer and winter here we have a never failing supply. At the White Mountains there is none, and without it we get sick."

The plant that Eskiminzin is referring to is the agave cactus. The tribes around Tucson had cultivated this plant for food for over two thousand years. Perhaps the Apaches learned how to cultivate and prepare the agave for food from the Pima and Papago tribes. The agave cactus looks somewhat like an overgrown artichoke. The Apaches would cut off its spiny leaves to get to the heart of it, similar to the way you eat the heart of an artichoke. Yet the agave cactus heart was bigger than a bowling ball. They would take many of these round hearts and roast them for several days underground or in a fire pit made of rocks. It was a soft, sweet, and nutritious food after several days. I was told by the San Carlos ethnobotanist Seth Pilsk that it tasted somewhat like a Bit-O-Honey candy bar.

Whitman told him that he had no authority to make a peace treaty with him or to promise his band a permanent sanctuary at Camp Grant, but if he would bring in his people he would feed them, until he was directed what to do by the Arizona Territory Department Commander, General George Stoneman. Notes in Whitman's journal state that on March 3, Eskiminzin arrived with his whole band. Other bands also began to arrive, and Whitman offered them the same terms, so that by March 5 there were three hundred Apaches at Camp Grant. In a short while, there were five hundred. Whitman did not require any of them to give up their weapons, as they were very poorly supplied with arms.[4]

When the people of Tucson received news of this arrangement they were outraged. The *Weekly Arizonian* newspaper of March 11, 1871, wrote a sarcastic and scathing article about Capitan Chiquito and Lieutenant Whitman clasping each other in an emotional embrace:

> Feed the murderers! Give them an opportunity to trade for and steal arms and ammunition! Clothe and protect them! Fawn upon them! Encourage them to new outrages! They have just gathered in their harvest of blood and need a short season of repose, and the sheltering arms of the fanatical Indian policy are ever ready to receive them. But it is not necessary that we advise or suggest further. All the hypocrites

and idiots have not died out yet—which in fact you will admit upon learning that a couple of hundred Apaches are feted and fawned upon at Camp Grant. Two weeks ago they applied to the commanding officer and were received with open arms. Quite natural: the Apache obeying his treacherous instincts and the officer obeying orders! But, oh, what an affectionate embrace! "Bloody Eye," alias "Capitan Chiquito" clasping the proud Caucasian to his brawny thorax, and the august magnate squeezing the clammy, naked savage against the gold buttons of his waistcoat, while the tears spurted from their eyes like water gushing through a knothole in the side of a bucket. It was a scene never to be forgotten; this meeting was. All nature [illegible] convulsed. The cats howled from sheer [illegible] and slapped each other around fearfully, [illegible] grunted, swine barked, and two Shanghai [illegible] commenced to gouge out each other's eyes [illegible]. There wasn't a dry eye in the neighborhood.[5]

That is an interesting nickname that the writer of this article had for Capitan Chiquito. I wonder if "Bloody Eye" was a name the people of Tucson often used for Capitan Chiquito.

In early April 1871, Captain Frank Stanwood arrived at Camp Grant to assume command. Lieutenant Whitman was relieved that General Stoneman had instructed Captain Stanwood to treat the Apaches as prisoners of war and to continue feeding them. Captain Stanwood "reported that four to five hundred Apaches were living at the rancheria, describing them as Aravaipas under Hashke Bahnzin [Eskiminzin], Pinals under Capitan Chiquito, and about 100 who were at Camp Goodwin a year ago."[6]

Captain Stanwood did not stay long at Camp Grant. After instructing Lieutenant Whitman to take a daily tally of each Apache male, he left for a prolonged patrol of southern Arizona with most of the troops of the post on April 24. He left Lieutenant Whitman in a vulnerable position with about fifty men to protect the Apache rancheria.[7]

As the season progressed and lower Aravaipa Creek turned foul and dried up, Lieutenant Whitman gave his permission to the Apaches to relocate five miles upstream where the springs kept the water pure and flowing. Doctor Conant Briesly, who became Camp Grant's medical officer just days before the massacre, testified that between April 25 and 30:

I saw the Indians every day. They seem very well contented, and were busily employed in bringing in hay, which they sold for manta and such little articles as they desired outside the government ration. April 29,

Capitan Chiquito and some of the other chiefs were at the post, and asked for seeds and some hoes, stating that they had ground cleared and ready for planting. They were told that the garden seeds had been sent for, and would be up from Tucson in a few days.[8]

On this same day Lieutenant Whitman made this entry in his journal about an encounter with Capitan Chiquito:

> Saturday 29th. Captain Chiquito in trouble about his favorite wife. Spoke sharply to her and she suddenly disappeared. He had looked for her all day and finally came to me. As he said to "lay his whole heart bare before me." I advised him as well as I could and expressed my sympathy for him. I never have seen any man in any grade of society express more anxious concern than he did, or in a more delicate way. He evidently loves her very much. I only hope he will get her back. Was very much gratified at this new evidence of entire confidence in me. . . . I do have great hopes for their future if they can be properly treated.[9]

The events of the following day, Sunday April 30, would change the lives of Capitan Chiquito and Lieutenant Whitman forever.

Yet there were still Apache raids going on in the Tucson area, and the citizens were convinced that they were by the Apaches from Camp Grant. The mission of San Xavier del Bac was attacked on April 10, and many cattle and horses of the Papago were driven off. A group of citizens and Papagos went on a fifty-mile chase, recovering most of the animals and killing one Apache. The settlement of San Pedro, about thirty miles upriver from Camp Grant, was attacked three days later and one settler was killed. Those who chased after the raiders ran into a large war party of Apaches, who killed three of their pursuers.

The headlines of the *Arizona Citizen* newspaper read:

> "Encouragement for murder! The Camp Grant Truce a Cruel Farce." The article stated that there was "no reasonable doubt but that Camp Grant–fed Indians made the raid on St. Xavier last Monday and because they were followed, punished and deprived of their plunder, they went to Grant, rested on Wednesday, and in stronger force on Thursday attacked the San Pedro settlement."[10]

Once again Jesus Maria Elias planned a revenge attack on the Aravaipa Apache, employing a similar strategy as the one he had used eight years before: attack with stealth and surprise on the sleeping Apache at dawn. The second in command of Jesus's war party was a man by the name of Bill Oury. Oury had served in the Texas Army during the revolution. He used to tell people that he was sent out from the Alamo just six days before its fall with a desperate message for help to Sam Houston. After the revolution he had joined the Texas Rangers and fought in several Indian engagements and also served in the Mexican-American war as a private in a company of Texas Mounted Rangers.[11]

On April 28, 1871, a group of men from Tucson arrived at their agreed-on rendezvous point about eight miles north of Tucson. There were 146 men in Jesus's Army of Revengers. There were ninety-two Papago from the San Xavier del Bac mission, some of them armed with firearms, but most with bows and arrows, war clubs and knives. The forty-eight Mexicans and six Anglos were armed with Sharps and Spencer rifles. They began their march north along the banks of the San Pedro River. When they neared Camp Grant they rode to the east and then north to avoid being seen and arrived at Aravaipa Creek with the Apache rancheria about two miles to the east of them, and Camp Grant about three miles to their West.[12]

Lieutenant Whitman had promised the Apache a fiesta and barbecue on the first of May. The Apache camp was enthusiastically preparing for the coming festivities. Several small parties of men were out hunting and gathering mescal for the feast. There were social dances being held in anticipation of the celebration. Dancing went on late into the night.[13] Capitan Chiquito was one of those who had gone out to hunt, but according to the Tucsonans, he had gone out on a raid.[14]

Leaving their horses about two miles away from the Apache rancheria, the war party advanced on foot in silence upstream. The Papagos led by Bill Oury and Chief Francisco provided the larger north wing of the line, and the Mexicans and the Anglos the southern wing. Jesus Elias was in the center of the formation in order to be able to give orders to either force. The Papago wing surrounded the sleeping Apache in their wickiups on three sides. The Mexicans and Anglos were in positions on top of the bluffs with their rifles, ready to shoot down any Apache who chose that route of escape.

Jesus had instructed the Papago that war clubs and knives only be used early in the raid in order to delay widespread alarm. Oury waited as two Papagos crept silently up the bluff to club two Apache sentries by a fire playing cards. With this accomplished he raised his arm and made a motion to go forward. Sweeping through the village the raiders took the sleeping Apaches completely by surprise. The Papago entered each wickiup and silently, brutally crushed the skulls of sleeping women with war clubs, and with razor-sharp knife blades slashed the throats of children in their sleep. The Apache awakened to a horrible nightmare. Some of the Apache girls were raped before being killed. Those along the bluff shot down those who ran, as they attempted to find safety in the hills to the south. The Apache who did manage to escape had slipped through the advancing Papago line, splashed across the Aravaipa Creek, and ran into the security of the rising hills to the north. Bodies were stripped, bullets and arrows were shot into corpses, and nearly all the dead were mutilated. Surviving children were rounded up and gathered in a group. Men went from wickiup to wickiup setting them on fire with torches and burning all stores of food. The whole job was done in about thirty minutes. Jesus signaled to the men on the bluff to move slowly down the hill in their skirmish line into the burning bodies strewn throughout the remains of the Apache camp. They fired bullets into the bodies spread about the rancheria to make certain they were dead. Then Jesus ordered his force to pull out and return to where the horses waited.[15]

One of the Apache survivors of the massacre, Sherman Curley (Chiquito's nephew), describes the following day as follows:

> The next day one man went back to the place where we had been dancing. He found lots of bodies of dead Apaches there. Some of the women and girls who had long, nice hair, they had cut a round place right out of the scalp, leaving the hair on, and taking it away with them. I don't know why they did this. This man came back, and told about it. Next day, the people who had gotten away, and were hidden in different places over the mountains, started to call one another together. When they had all gathered they sent that same man who had been back to the dance ground, and fifteen others, down towards Camp Grant. When they were near the camp, they stopped, and rested on some level ground. Then their two headman, Capitan Chiquito and Hashke Bahnzin [Eskiminzin] went and talked with the agent [Whitman], telling him all that had happened. The officer said that those Mexicans and Papagos would never come back, and that even if they did, the soldiers there at Camp Grant would know about it first. The officer said that up until this time they had been good friends, and had gotten along all right. This is why he had sent out for them to come in and talk. He sent men up to bury the dead for the Apaches, and he gave out rations to those who had

survived. He told them to come back, and settle down again. The band did so, and made their camp on the Aravaipa River, about one mile from the soldiers, so they would be near them, and have protection.[16]

When Lieutenant Whitman received word of the massacre he offered a one hundred dollar reward to whoever would go into the hills and explain to the Apaches that his soldiers had nothing to do with this horrible deed. There were no takers. He sent the post surgeon Dr. Briesly with a wagon and about twenty men to bring back the wounded, but Briesly found there was no use for medicine, as the work had been too thoroughly done. Almost one-fourth of the camp had been killed for a total of 125, more or less. Of these only eight were men, the rest were women and children. Whitman stated that the cries of the women were "too wild and terrible to be described." He sent horses into the mountains that brought back two wounded women, one shot through the left lung and one with an arm shattered. The one with the shattered arm was the wife of Capitan Chiquito. Both women later recovered. There were twenty-nine Apache children taken captive. Of these, two managed to escape and five were later returned from Arizona citizens. The other twenty-two were taken to Sonora and sold.[17]

According to the daughter of Jesus Elias, Alvina Rosenda:

Father brought home a captive, a young girl about eighteen. He was about to shoot her when she called to him in Spanish, "Don't kill me. I am not an Indian. I am a captive." Father saved her and set her up on a cliff and put his own hat on her head so that the other men would not shoot her. She was dressed as the Indian and was somewhat tanned but naturally she was very good-looking with gray eyes and a clear complexion. She said that she had been a captive only about a week. That the Indians had attacked her father's ranch in Mexico and killed all of her family and taken her captive. She was only with us a short time when a man came up looking for her. Mother told her to go into the room but did not tell her why, and when she saw the man, she burst out crying. He was the Mexican girl's brother-in-law, and he took her home with him. Many of the men brought back captives but most of them were later returned to the reservation. Jimmie Lee brought back two which he gave to his sister, Mrs. R. G. Brady and she raised them. They were later married to Mexicans and the daughter of one of them is now chambermaid at the Congress Hotel. The captives who were not returned stayed of their own will and not because they were forced to. Capitan Chiquito was one of the chiefs of the Aravaipa Apache, a little dark man but very brave. I do not think that he was the one who aimed the gun at my father which did not go off, because as I have always understood it, Capitan was off on a raiding expedition at the time. It was only the old men, women, and children left at the camp. When Capitan returned home he found that both of his wives had been killed and he was very angry and tried to get revenge. So he took ninety men and went on another raid, I think out near San Xavier, and did great robbery and drove off much stock. My father and uncles and a few neighbors followed them but there were only ten or twelve Mexicans and when they found out how many Indians there were they gave up the chase. So the Indians got all the stock.[18]

This claim was substantiated in the 1888 Court of Claims by Juan Elias versus the United States and Apache Indians, Indian Depredations. Juan claimed that he lost fifty head of cattle on a raid of San Xavier by the Apache in April 1871, and only recovered seven. Juan was awarded $21,650 by the United States Court of Claims for all of the cattle and horses stolen from him by the Apache over the course of his lifetime.[19]

Apache Revenge and Peace Talks with the Americans

FOUR DAYS AFTER THE massacre of the Apache people near Camp Grant, a group of one hundred Apache warriors under the Chiricahua Chief Juh finally obtained revenge on an army officer who had killed many of their people. His name was Lieutenant Howard Bass Cushing. Chief Juh had a long-standing hatred for Cushing following an incident in the Guadalupe Mountains of New Mexico, when Troop F had attacked a Mescalero Apache camp. In this massacre many women and children were killed similar to the slaughter at Camp Grant. Chief Juh had also heard much about Lieutenant Cushing's depredations in Arizona. He murdered people up around Camp Grant and Globe (Besh be gowah). He attacked and killed many Indians at night. They were not of the Chiricahua band, but they were considered brothers. The scouts of Juh were watching Cushing and tracking him. West of the town of Tombstone, Juh finally maneuvered Cushing into an ambush. He lured the officer into a canyon by sending one of the women up a dry arroyo so that the soldiers might follow her. Chief Juh was not interested in killing all the soldiers of Troop F of the United States Cavalry, he just wanted to kill Cushing.[1] Cushing foolishly pursued a band of Apaches of over one hundred warriors, and the Apaches lay down a devastating hail of fire. Cushing was first shot in the chest and cried out, "Sergeant, I am killed!

Take me out! Take me out!" When two of Cushing's men tried to drag their fallen leader toward the horses, Cushing was shot mortally in the head. The soldiers had to abandon Cushing and flee for their lives.[2]

Survivors of the Camp Grant Massacre slowly began to return to Aravaipa and set up camp along the Creek. This time they built their wickiups closer to the fort, and they believed in Lieutenant Whitman's assurances of protection.[3] Whitman wrote the following in his journal on May 27 about the return of Capitan Chiquito and other Apaches:

> Indians came in 190, over 90 men. Only about 12 of Captain Chiquito's band. Few men from the other part of the same band came in and had a long talk with the Captain. A fine looking and intelligent man, and only asks the same privileges as are given the others. . . . Am myself entirely confident that my efforts in behalf of these people will be rewarded.[4]

Yet in early June this second fragile peace was broken, and this time it was by American soldiers. A cavalry patrol from Fort Apache to the north came into Aravaipa Canyon while hunting deer. The troops were startled when they ran into a band of Apaches, among them Eskiminzin, and they open fired on the Apaches. An Apache warrior named Muna-clee was killed. Eskiminzin considered the days of peace between the Aravaipa and the white men were over, and Eskiminzin told Lieutenant Whitman that the promise to his people was broken and that he was leaving Camp Grant. He told Whitman, "We now go back to the mountains to avenge our dead."[5]

A few days later:

> Eskiminzin visited a longtime friend of his, Charles McKinney, a 35-year-old Irish man who farmed near Camp Grant on the San Pedro. McKinney invited the Apache to share his supper with him and Eskiminzin accepted. Over the meal there was talk and laughter. Yes, things had been bad for them, the chief told his white friend, but they would soon be better. When the meal was done McKinney poured more coffee for both, and they remained at the table, talking, drinking their coffee, and smoking cigarettes made from McKinney's paper and tobacco. When it was time for him to leave, Eskiminzin stood, and thanked his host for the meal, for the hospitality, the good conversation. Calmly, then, the Apache drew a revolving pistol from his belt, aimed it at the startled McKinney's head, and coolly pulled the trigger.[6]

This murder took place on June 8, 1871, according to Whitman's journal.

Early in July there was another opportunity for Eskiminzin to avenge the massacre of his people. Eskiminzin and his war chief, Capitan Chiquito, planned an attack on a wagon train on its way from Camp Lowell to Fort Bowie. The seven large wagons were hauled by five yoked oxen and were loaded with goods for the company store at Fort Bowie and with arms and ammunition and an assortment of other military supplies. The plan was to ambush the wagons as they crossed the dry bed at Cienega Wash. With a force of forty warriors, Eskiminzin would remain hidden in the hills between the point of ambush and the advance column troops. Capitan Chiquito and his smaller force, armed primarily with bows and arrows and lances rather than noisy rifles, would ambush the wagons as they crossed the creek bed. The Aravaipa needed the arms and ammunition and provisions. Capitan Chiquito's party attacked the wagons at Cienega Wash at a time when the infantry column was a mile ahead of the wagons. The plan misfired, however, for there were some soldiers concealed in the wagons who fought off the Apaches until the infantry could return on the double. Eskiminzin lost thirteen warriors.

Many of Capitan Chiquito's group were trapped in an arroyo by the returning infantry. Eskiminzin himself took a bullet through his left arm. As the Apaches ran to save themselves, the soldiers returned to the wagons and took stock of the situation. An army private by the name of Harris from Pennsylvania had died when an Apache bullet struck him in the cheek. They buried him on the roadside at the scene of the attack. One soldier and two teamsters were treated for minor wounds. Three oxen had been killed. For the next few months Eskiminzin and Capitan Chiquito remained with their followers in the Galiuro Mountains. In Don Schellie's account of this battle he calls Capitan Chiquito "Little Captain."[7]

In June 1871 General George Crook, who had distinguished himself in battle during the Civil War and proven himself a capable Indian fighter against the Paiutes, arrived in Tucson to replace General Stoneman as military commander of the Department of Arizona.

Worcester writes: "In his campaigns against the Paiutes Crook had gained fame while developing pursuit techniques that would serve him well in Arizona."[8] General Crook was ready to pursue an aggressive campaign using Apache scouts to fight the renegade Apache, as it was Crook's theory that the Apache must first be beaten militarily and then placed on reservations.

In regard to Crook's tactics, Dan L. Thrapp further comments: "From the outset Crook was convinced the Apaches were never going to be conquered by troops alone, nor by the civilians, nor even by some combination of troops and civilians. They would have to be beaten by their own people."[9] Crook moved quickly and quietly to put his plans into action as soon as possible, but then, quite unexpectedly, the military operation was stopped short.

President Ulysses Grant, no doubt displeased that a camp that bore his name was now well known as a massacre site of Apaches, gave to the secretary of the Board of Indian Commissioners, Vincent Colyer, the authority to select and create reservations. Grant also instructed the secretary of war to ensure that the army supported any agreement that Colyer might make with the Apaches. General Crook had to immediately suspend his Apache campaign when he heard of Colyer's mission.[10]

Vincent Colyer, the peacemaker from Washington, was forty-seven years old and by profession an artist well known for his paintings of the Southwest. While he was at Camp Grant he actually did a color landscape painting of the site of the Camp Grant Massacre, which is now held in the collection of the Houston Museum of Fine Arts.[11] However, much of his time was devoted to humanitarian pursuits. He had commanded and organized a Negro volunteer regiment during the Civil War.[12]

Lieutenant Whitman made a note in his journal on September 10, 1871:

> Garza, Ezkiminzin and about 100 men and women here fed today. Heard something from Capt. "Chiquito." Am sure he will be in a few days. Was told he was very angry with Ezkiminzin at his breaking the peace.[13]

Commissioner Colyer had arrived at Camp Grant on September 13, 1871. On September 16 there were 166 Apaches present at a distribution of clothing by Commissioner Colyer, and on the morning of September 19 there were seventy-nine more Apaches from the band of Capitan Chiquito given a distribution of clothing.[14]

At a meeting with the Apaches on September 15, Chief Eskiminzin told Colyer that at about four o'clock in the morning they were attacked and 128 were killed and twenty-nine children taken prisoner. He and all the captains lost some of their families. He lost two wives, four children, and two of his nephews were taken away. Commissioner Colyer asked:

"Does this country still please them after what has taken place?" And he was told, Yes! This has always been their home and the home of their fathers. Commissioner Colyer told them that they must not fight the Papagos or the white people anymore. He said he had already sent for the children, and when he got back to Washington he would ask the president to request the government of Mexico to return their children.[15]

Eskiminzin took Commissioner Colyer to the massacre site on September 17. There were still camp utensils, clothing, and blankets on the ground. They could still see skulls with their temples crushed in at the creek side. Colyer was moved by the tears in Eskiminzin's eyes at the sight of these ruins.[16]

Capitan Chiquito did not arrive at Camp Grant until September 19, according to the report of Vincent Colyer and the journal of Lieutenant Whitman. Commissioner Colyer sent out a distribution of food and clothing to his camp with an invitation to meet with him. The commissioner told Capitan Chiquito that he was glad that he had seen him before he left for Washington. Capitan Chiquito made a statement on September 19, which must have been more beautiful and poetic in his own language, but was translated by the interpreter as follows:

> He has nothing more to say than the other chiefs had said; He confirms
> all that they have said. He had heard that his father and mother had
> come and he asked to see them. The same God who rules the Sun, he
> believes, had sent me here to see them. Ever since the other Indians had
> told him that I was here, He wished to see me, and for that reason he
> had hurried in from the hills. It must have been God who had put it into
> both of our hearts to hurry to see each other. He thanks us for having
> sent him out food and clothing last night.[17]

Although Commissioner Colyer encouraged them to move to the reservation now established at Fort Apache, he eventually consented to their refusal to abandon their Aravaipa homeland, and he responded by creating a reserve for them in the vicinity of Camp Grant.[18]

The following December, 1871, the physician stationed at Camp Grant, Dr. Valery Havard, traveled up Aravaipa Creek from Camp Grant and found the two mass burial mounds of the Apache massacre victims. He apparently dug into the burial ground or found a previously buried skull exposed by floodwaters. The analysis done by the Smithsonian Museum determined that the skull had originally been buried.

The skull was that of a young adult female, perhaps twenty to thirty years old. Dr. Havard boxed up the remains and sent them to the Army Medical Museum for study. On the skull is written: "Apache skull, Aravaipa Tribe, Camp Grant, Arizona Territory: sent by acting assistant surgeon Valery Havard USA, December 15, 1871 from the ground of the massacre of April 30, 1871."[19]

I have several photos of this Apache woman's skull that I requested from the Smithsonian, but after consulting with several of my Apache friends I have decided that it would not be respectful to make them public.

This strange deed that the doctor carried out was actually in accordance with orders from the surgeon general's office at the time. This directive called on military medical officers to collect crania together with specimens of Indian weapons, dress, implements, diet, and medicines. Havard was a Frenchman who studied medicine in Paris before immigrating to the United States. He was for a time the house physician in Children's Hospital and professor of French, chemistry, and botany at Manhattan College. In 1871 he was appointed as assistant surgeon in the army and commissioned as assistant surgeon in the Medical Corps. After his time in Arizona he served in the Spanish-American War and was in the field during the battle of San Juan Hill. In 1904 he was detailed as a medical attaché with the Russian Army in Manchuria during the Russian-Japanese War, and was taken captive by the Japanese. Taken to Japan, he was eventually released for return to the United States. He also served in World War I, where he received the Cuban Order of Military Merit. At the age of eighty-one he died on board the steamship *Columbo* while returning from a visit to France. He wrote many books, including *The Manual of Military Hygiene, Report on the Flora of Western and Southern Texas, Notes on the Trees of Cuba,* and many other pamphlets on botanical and medical subjects.[20]

There were legends that the Aravaipa Apache possessed a rich mine from which they secured the gold to carry on their trading, which was located about ten miles northwest of their rancheria in Aravaipa.[21] Woodworth Clum, writing from the notes of his father, John Clum, states that about this time (perhaps December 1871) it was reported that Capitan Chiquito killed an American who was searching for gold.[22] Perhaps this was true, yet I find that the Indian agent John Clum always paints Eskiminzin to be a peace-loving Indian chief and does not mention incidences like his killing of Charles McKenny. Clum's notes even say that Eskiminzin went to see Indian Commissioner Vincent Colyer by himself, as he feared for the safety of the rest of his tribe. However, John Clum was not in Arizona at this time, but Lieutenant Whitman was, and Whitman writes in his journal notes that Capitan Chiquito "was very angry with Ezkiminzin at his breaking the peace."[23]

President Grant approved the orders given to General Crook to wage a vigorous campaign against the Apache. Yet under pressures from the peace party, and his own conscience, he wrote:

> I do not believe that our Creator ever placed different races of men
> on this earth with the view of having the stronger exert all of their
> energies on exterminating the weaker. If any change takes place in
> the Indian policy of the government while I hold my present office it
> will be on the humanitarian side of the question.[24]

Grant decided that a new effort should be made to induce all the Apache by persuasive means to settle on the reservation. He sent a representative of the Department of the Interior to Arizona to cooperate with the military in preserving peace and to expedite the execution of the government's new policy. The man chosen for the mission was General Oliver Otis Howard, known by many as "Bible quoting Howard," a veteran officer with a distinguished combat record, a champion of the underprivileged, and a deeply religious man. Howard arrived at Fort McDowell in April 1872.

Crook wrote of Howard: "General Howard is fond of public speaking. His themes generally were 'how he was converted' and 'the battle of Gettysburg.'" Howard had lost his right arm in a battle in the Civil War. Crook said that he was very amused of the "general's opinion of himself. He told me that he thought the creator had placed them on earth to be the Moses to the Negro. Having accomplish[ed] this mission, he felt satisfied that his next mission was with the Indian."[25]

And Howard wrote of Crook: "The general had that art which some men possess of saying very little to you in conversation, being at the same time such an attentive listener that one was unconsciously drawn out in discourse."[26]

I believe that the Apache respected General Crook because he had some humility and had no grandiose ideas about his importance. General Howard, on the other hand, they would probably refer to as an *indaa adilkaa*: a person who considers himself superior to others and is haughty and pretentious. The Apache felt that the white man in general was lacking in modesty and humility and had an attitude of imperiousness and condensation when dealing with other people.

Another term the Apache have for the white man is *indaa dogoyaada*: a white man who is lacking in wisdom and understanding. They felt that white men lack self-awareness, a form of ignorance that blinds them to the effects of their actions on other people.[27]

I tried not to be an *indaa adilkaa* when I worked in the San Carlos emergency room. We were taught not to look Apache women directly in the eyes, as this was considered too forward, rude, and direct. We had to learn to be sensitive and respectful in our intake screening when we had to ask required federal questions such as: When was your last menstrual period? Do you have problems with alcohol? Is there domestic violence in your home? After a number of years, I learned to walk the way of Apache courtesy, etiquette, and respect.

At Fort McDowell on April 18, 1872, General Howard wrote:

Chiquito is chief of the Pinals who were here. Dr. Bendell, Indian superintendent, just in from Camp Grant, reports Chiquito now at that place. He had a conversation with him there. These facts seem to indicate that the Indians have left the reservation more from dissatisfaction than from a desire to enter upon hostilities. I recommend that the rations furnished by the Indian Bureau to the Sioux be allowed for these reservations.[28]

In an informal meeting with Santo at Camp Grant on April 24, 1871, General Howard asked Santo, the medicine man of the Aravaipa, "Do you think it is right to steal horses?" Santo replied, "It is right when there are no friends anywhere. It seems as if there is a difference. God puts us here, and we have no clothes and but little food, but you come here with plenty of clothes and food and good things." General Howard tried to tell them about the Bible: "The Bible says we should love one another." Santo the medicine man replied, "That is what we want. We want to do right. We're talking now where Almighty God hears us. We thank you." General Howard replied, "Good men love, bad men hate. Do you know what a thought is?" Santo replied, "It is what I see in the heart, sometimes I do not see it." General Howard said, "God is like a thought. He loves every body." And the medicine man replied, "It must be that he likes the Mexicans and Americans better than he does us. He has given them all good things, and he has not given us anything."[29]

General Howard took a great liking to this medicine man of the Aravaipa, Chief Santo. He said, "I took a glance at Santo, as he sat upon a small bench looking at me. He had rather a long body, short legs, and a very large head. His face was so honest that it occurred to me to try an experiment. Accordingly I told Conception [my Apache interpreter] to say to him, 'You have a father up yonder,' pointing upward. He seemed pleasantly to assent. I said next: 'I, General Howard, have a father up there too. Your father and my father are the same. Then if you and I have the same father, we must be brothers. Santo rose at once and came to place his hand in mine. He was so sincere that from that time until his death he was my devoted friend. Without him I could not have accomplished what I did with our Aravaipa Apaches at the meeting.'"[30]

A year after the massacre on May 20, General Howard held a peace conference at Camp Grant with an astonishing group of former enemies, including Capitan Chiquito, Eskiminzin, Lieutenant Whitman, General George Crook, Arizona governor Anson Safford, Jesus Elias, Bill Oury, Chief Antonio of the Akimel O'odham, and Chief Francisco of the Tohono O'odham. Lasting several days, the talks focused on reconciling the factions and, because of Apache insistence, repatriating the captive children.[31]

At the beginning of the meeting of General Howard at Camp Grant, the "praying general" fell to his knees and begged God to strengthen them in this undertaking. The Apaches were terrified of this, believing that he was making evil magic, and they ran and hid themselves in various places. Eskiminzin at some point peered around the side of a building and motioned to Lieutenant Whitman. Whitman reassured him of the general's good intentions and that he was not placing curses on them.

The meeting began with words from Apache Chief Santo, followed by a longer speech from Eskiminzin. Chief Antonio of the Akimel O'odham (Pima) voiced optimism of a peace with the Apache. Tohono O'odham (Papago) Chief Francisco, who had led his tribe at the Camp Grant Massacre, was also cautiously optimistic that peace could be obtained with the Apache. However, Governor Safford was doubtful that any agreement they came to at this meeting would prevent raids by renegade Indians.

Jesus Elias, the leader of two raids on the Aravaipa Apache, advised the Apaches to "be careful to obey the orders of your general and the officers placed over you. This is for your welfare. You must not believe that the government, which is over me as well as over you, does not possess the power and soldiers and money, to compel your obedience." Eskiminzin took exception to Elias's veiled threat, declaring that the Apaches had satisfactorily expressed their commitment to peace and protesting this attempt to intimidate them. Elias responded, "Have I not told Eskiminzin and Capitan Chiquito that the government has the power to destroy you all, but that it does not want to do so, but wants to save you and have you live as other people live." He then declared himself satisfied with the Apaches' sincerity.[32]

Capitan Chiquito did not arrive until the last day of the meeting, May 23, but he agreed with the peace agreements that had been made. General Howard said he wanted to talk much more with Eskiminzin and Chiquito before he went away, and he wanted Eskiminzin to go with him to look at the place for a new reservation.[33]

Before General Howard left Arizona he wanted to take a delegation of Aravaipa and White Mountain Apaches with him to Washington, DC. None of the Aravaipa chiefs would agree to go, except the medicine man, Santo. Santo met President Grant and was given a medal that said, "On Earth Peace. Good Will Towards Men. 1871." On his return to San Carlos, General Howard gave Santo his bible. For the rest of his life, Santo kept this bible under his head as he slept.[34]

Some of General Howard's comments about Chief Eskiminzin are interesting yet somewhat puzzling. In the stories we hear of Eskiminzin, he is noted several times to give long speeches, yet General Howard refers to him as "Eskiminzin the stammerer." Howard stated that Eskiminzin stuttered so badly that it was hard to understand him. He related one story when Eskiminzin was speaking to the Apache interpreter Concepcion. Concepcion struggled to understand him and finally gave up. He said, "Eskiminzin no talk good, me no Savey." They then called Santo to speak for Eskiminzin. Howard noted that at this meeting Santo stated that he was once chief of their band, and when he became old he made his son-in-law Eskiminzin chief of their band. It was his son-in law who brought their band to Aravaipa Canyon. Perhaps the stuttering of Eskiminzin was a temporary condition for him after the shock and trauma of losing wives and children at the massacre at Camp Grant.[35]

General Howard left Camp Grant on May 25 after he had first established a new reservation in an area farther north where water was more abundant and future raids from the people of Tucson were less likely. I can imagine that Capitan Chiquito vowed that he would one day return to live in Aravaipa, the land of his birth.

Capitan Chiquito and Eskiminzin led their followers north in February 1873 to the new reserve General Howard had created for them. This place was at the intersection of the San Carlos and Gila Rivers, and is known today as the San Carlos Apache Reservation.[36]

This place would be the main settlement of the Apaches at San Carlos for over fifty years, yet it is known now as "Old San Carlos." Before the completion of the Coolidge Dam in 1930, the buildings at Old San Carlos were blown up with dynamite and a large cement slab placed over the cemetery. The waters of what is now San Carlos Lake slowly began to rise and covered what was once the village. Most Apache people moved up the San Carlos River to a place then known as Rice. This is the location of the present town of San Carlos; it is where the hospital was that I worked at for twenty-one years. Rice Elementary School in San Carlos is named after Lieutenant Sedgewick Rice who was the San Carlos Indian agent in 1897. The foundations of the buildings at Old San Carlos can sometimes be seen when the lake waters recede in times of drought. A memorial was placed at Old San Carlos about ten years ago with statues of an Apache family praying to the Creator with their arms raised over the tombstone of one of their dead. The road that goes by Old San Carlos and to the lake was once the site of many automobile accidents. My very first day working in the emergency room I had the unpleasant task of taking a young man's body to the morgue whose car had rolled over on the lake road. Some Apache people told me that the spirits of the dead under the lake would sometimes grab a steering wheel of a passing car to have that person join them. A more likely explanation is that they were going to or from the lake store, which was once the only place on the reservation where you could buy beer.

Yet, before this exodus from Aravaipa to Old San Carlos took place, Capitan Chiquito, Eskiminzin, and other Aravaipa Apaches assisted General Crook and the United States Army in another slaughter.

8

The Battle of Skull Cave and the Mystery of the Medal of Honor

GENERAL CROOK HAD COOPERATED fully with the peace missions of Vincent Colyer and General Howard, even though he always believed that these missions would be largely a waste of time. The peace missions, however, had placed many hundreds of Indians on various reservations that Colyer and Howard had helped to establish. Nevertheless, there were still thousands of Indians who had not yet settled on any reservation and would not willingly do so. There were many Indian attacks and despoilments throughout that year of 1872, especially being carried out by the Yavapai. Because of these continuing hostilities, even the people back east were now convinced that Crook's offensive was long overdue. In his annual report for 1872 Crook writes:

> I think I am justified in saying that I've fully carried out that portion
> of my instructions which required me to cooperate with the agents
> referred to, and believe that humanity demands that I should now pro-
> ceed to carry out the remainder of my instructions, which require me to
> punish the incorrigibly hostile.[1]

Crook began to enlist Apache scouts at Fort Apache and then went on south to Camp Grant where he recruited more scouts, including Chief Eskiminzin, and most probably Capitan Chiquito. The drive from Fort Apache today to the place where Camp Grant once stood is a beautiful one over rolling hills. You travel from an elevation of over 6,000 feet and pine forests to an elevation of about 2,500 feet with saguaro cactus and semiarid desert. The highway today makes this an awesome and scenic drive, yet traveling overland on horseback as General Crook did must have been a formidable task. It took Crook four days to make this trip. Today it is about a two-hour drive.

Crook's instructions to the troops were simple and straightforward, as recorded by one of his officers, Captain John Bourke:

> Indians should be induced to surrender in all cases where possible; where they preferred to fight, they were to get all the fighting they wanted, and in one good dose instead of a number of petty engagements, but in either case were to be hunted down until the last one in hostility has been killed or captured. Every effort should be made to avoid the killing of women and children. Prisoners of either sex should be guarded from ill-treatment of any kind. When prisoners could be induced to enlist as scouts, they should be so enlisted, because the wilder the Apache was, the more he was likely to know the wiles and stratagems of those still out in the mountains, their hiding places and intentions. No excuse was to be accepted for leaving a trail; if horses played out, the enemies must be followed on foot, and no sacrifice should be left untried to make the campaign short, sharp, and decisive.[2]

Capitan Chiquito and Eskiminzin had a bad reputation among the US Army and the people of Tucson for their many depredations, yet Crook was willing to forget the past if the Apache scouts would assist him in conquering or gaining the cooperation of other Apache bands. Historian Charles M. Robinson writes:

> Crook left Camp Apache on December 3, and arrived at Camp Grant four days later. He held a council with Indians, similar to the one held at Camp Apache. Among those present was Eskiminzin, who promised to aid in hunting down the hostiles. Crook detested the idea of dealing with "Old Skimmy"; nevertheless, thirty one Apaches enlisted as scouts. A day later, ten more signed up.[3]

As the troops and Apache scouts left Camp Grant, their main objective was to find the camps of the Yavapai chiefs, Chuntz and Delshay, thought to be in the Fort Peaks range. Captain John Bourke recalls: "Chuntz had recently murdered in cold blood, at Camp Grant, a Mexican boy too young to have been the cause of rancor to anyone.[4]

Although many southwestern writers refer to this campaign as being one against the Tonto Apaches, these people were not Apache at all, but Yavapai. The Yavapai did not speak the Athabascan language of the Apache; they spoke an Uto-Aztecan language. Although I have found no record of it, I am assuming that Capitan Chiquito was part of this campaign, based on his close association with Ezkiminzin, with whom he was "joined at the hip," and the hostilities directed toward Capitan Chiquito by the Yavapai, when they were later brought to San Carlos, which I will speak of later.

Crook's soldiers and Apache scouts were able to find and destroy the rancheria of Chuntz with a very full winter stock of food, yet, Chuntz and his whole band escaped, due to the alarm given by a female Indian who had discovered the advance of the scouts. One of the Apache scouts, Nantaje, said he knew of the cave where a large band of Yavapai would be. Nantaje said he would take the US troops there at the first appearance of a star on the eastern horizon that would help him locate the cave. This star was most certainly Sirius, the Dog Star, that rises brightly in the east about 8:00 p.m. in December in San Carlos. I often saw Sirius brilliantly shining in the eastern sky at dusk from my backyard in San Carlos.

The soldiers and Apaches descended into the Salt River Canyon on Christmas Day. It was no doubt a clear and starry night. The Salt River Canyon is awesome and beautiful and is called by some Arizonians "the little Grand Canyon." I once took a rafting trip with Velma and her sister, Deana, down this canyon. The views are magnificent, yet there are many dangers, especially if you are walking along the banks at night. Bourke records that they lost one mule to a rattlesnake. As they advanced up the Salt River Canyon, they were becoming nervous and doubtful that any large group of Yavapai could live in this place. Nantaje just smiled and said, "Wait and see."[5]

They reached the cave in the early morning light of December 27, 1872. The Yavapai position seemed impregnable. The cave was one thousand feet above the Salt River with a natural rampart of sandstone ten feet high in front to provide ample protection to the Indians. The canyon was surrounded on both sides by the army, then the Apaches and army troops took positions with their rifles behind boulders that concealed them in front of the cave. The Yavapai were asked twice to surrender their women and children with promises that no harm would befall them, but they were confident of their ability to defend themselves, and they answered with cries of scorn. The soldiers sent volleys of fire directed on the mouth of the cave. The acoustics of the canyon magnified the blast of every gunshot. For three minutes soldiers shot into the cave as rapidly as they could. Although they could not see the Indians directly, they soon learned that they could ricochet their shots off the top of the cave into the mass of men below it. The Yavapai attempted one or two charges outside of the cave but were forced to retreat by their outnumbered forces. The soldiers then charged the cave, but there was little resistance, as they found seventy-six men lying dead, and thirty-five wounded woman and children. The cave was found full of supplies, with food and ammunition taken on recent raids. After the Salt River battle the troops took the captives to Fort McDowell.[6]

Several of the Apache scouts who took part in the Salt River battle were awarded congressional Medals of Honor at the recommendation of General Crook. Among those to receive this honor was the Apache guide Nantaje and several other Apache scouts. One of these scouts was Chiquito. Although Chiquito is listed as a Sierra Blanca (White Mountain Apache), the bands to whom the Apaches belonged were often confused by the US Army. Capitan Chiquito is sometimes called Chief of the Pinals, or an Aravaipa chief, and he is often confused with Capitan Chiquito of the White Mountain band. Although there are records of Chiquito enlisting as an Apache scout in subsequent campaigns, there is no record of him enlisting at Camp Grant, but neither is there any record of the enlistment of other Medal of Honor recipients, such as Machol or Blanquet.

There is some archaeological evidence that leans in Capitan Chiquito of Aravaipa's favor: the Medal of Honor was found in the Wheatfields, north of Globe, in an area once farmed by the Aravaipa and Pinal bands. This area was once known as the "Pinal Maizefields." This is on the San Carlos Reservation side of the Salt River, and not the White Mountain Reservation side, north of the Salt River.

One of the survivors of this battle was an eight-year-old boy named Hoomothya. Hoomothya later wrote a book called *All My People Were Killed*. He writes in his book: "All of my people were killed in a cave by the soldiers and by Indian scouts enlisted by the government. This was in 1872. There lived in this cave on the north side of the Salt River 225 souls—men, women, and poor innocent children who were slaughtered like cattle."[7]

The man who now owns Chiquito's Medal of Honor acquired it from some men, who with metal detectors found it near a burned out home in the Wheatfields. He gave a photo of the medal to the Arizona Historical Society, but it is still in his possession. My wife, Velma, and I once visited this man's home near Prescott. He was a kindly older man who took a liking to the sweetness and innocence that Velma could often project (those who knew Velma more intimately were well aware of the iron will and thunder that she possessed). Velma's spirit animal was the turtle: a reptile that moves forward cautiously, slowly, but with great resolution and determination. Like the turtle, Velma carried a hard shell to defend herself, and if you prodded her, she would draw inside tightly into this impregnable fortress of shell. If you were not careful, she would snap at you with a bite that would never let go.

That kind man in Prescott was intrigued that Velma was Capitan Chiquito's great-granddaughter, and he invited us into his home and showed us all the artifacts that he had collected in his years of scouting the Southwest. Yet he did not share with us Chiquito's congressional Medal of Honor, which, he said, he had in a safety deposit box. He did later send us, however, photos of Skull Cave and directions on how to get there, if we ever chose to visit the site. Velma and I asked him if he would consider donating the medal to the San Carlos Apache Tribe, or to the Arizona Historical Society, but he evaded our requests. I am sure that he is aware that there is a federal law against buying or selling congressional Medals of Honor.

Velma and I never visited Skull Cave, but we did visit the Fort McDowell Cemetery, where the bones of the Yavapai killed at Skull Cave had been taken and buried in a mass grave. The memorial stone at the grave site reads: "In Remembrance of the Brave Yavapai Men, Women, and Children Who Were Massacred at the Skeleton Cave December 1872, by the US Army." I can still see Velma praying over the grave with her arms held up to the sky. She did not share her prayer with me, but I'm sure it included a plea for forgiveness for whatever part her great-grandfather had in the deaths of these people.

Troubles on the San Carlos Apache Reservation and Adventures with John Clum

AFTER THE BATTLE OF Skull Cave, the US Army placed the two opposing Indian tribes together at San Carlos, somehow expecting that "everything would be just fine." Yet Eskiminzin and Capitan Chiquito had just assisted the army with the destruction of the Yavapai Chief Chuntz's rancheria and the massacre of his tribal members at Skull Cave. Some 1,500 Apache and Yavapai were thrown together at San Carlos. John Upton Terrell writes:

> There serious troubles arose. The most turbulent spirits of all the Apache who had survived the campaign were now thrown together. Conflicts for leadership began. Two major factions soon evolved, one led by a Eskiminzin and Chiquito, the other by Chuntz, Cochinay, and Bacoon—all desperados, and all diehards who had never accepted in their hearts the peace that had been forced upon them. Violence frequently occurred. Chiquito's favorite wife was sexually attacked by a Chuntz partisan. Heads were smashed. One of Chuntz's followers shot and killed a warrior of Eskiminzin's band. Moreover, although they were fighting each other, all the leaders threatened to break out if two companies of cavalry stationed on the reservation were not removed.[1]

The experiment at San Carlos was the beginning of a calculated plan by the United States to destroy the Apache culture and to somehow assimilate the Apaches into mainstream America. Some Apache today refer to San Carlos as an Apache concentration camp. Their nomadic and free way of existence, and their hunting and gathering lifestyle, was to be replaced by army rations and a total dependence on the government. No more would the Apaches live on seeds and nuts and berries; these would be replaced by army rations of flour, salt, beef, and lard. Most Apaches today think of "Indian fry bread" as being a traditional food, yet this was a creation brought about by the rations that were allowed them.

When General Howard chose the land that was to become the San Carlos Apache Reservation, having a stable source of water was a prime concern, yet this was not an area known for abundant wildlife and edible plant life. The most prominent mountain near the town site was named by the Americans "Mount Triplet" after its three peaks. However, the Apache name for the mountain is Doo ya'init'an, which means "Nothing grows there." Decades later, Asa Daklugie, the son of Chief Juh, in retrospect exclaimed:

> San Carlos! That was the worst place in all the great territory stolen
> from the Apaches. If anybody had ever lived there permanently, no
> Apache knew of it. . . . Nearly all of the vegetation was cacti; and though
> in season a little cactus fruit was produced, the rest of the year food
> was lacking. The heat was terrible. The insects were terrible. The water
> was terrible. . . . Insects and rattlesnakes seem to thrive there. . . . There
> were also tarantulas, Gila monsters, and centipedes. . . . At times it was
> so hot that I am sure a thermometer would have registered well above
> 120 degrees.[2]

The Apache were not alone in their feelings about San Carlos. Lieutenant Britton Davis, who was assigned to San Carlos in 1882, referred to it as Hell's Forty Acres.

> Scrawny, dejected lines of scattered cottonwoods, shrunken, almost
> leafless, marked the course of the streams. Rain was so infrequent that
> it took on the semblance of a phenomenon when it came at all. Almost
> continuously, dry, hot, dust- and gravel-laden winds swept the plain, de-
> nuding it of every vestige of vegetation. In summer a temperature of 110
> in the shade was cool weather.[3]

Having lived twenty-one years at San Carlos, I will have to say that I loved it. Of course, we have air conditioning now. I love the quietness and the solitude of the semiarid desert. Some sunsets and sunrises are glorious. I have never seen the Milky Way or the stars so crisply and clearly in any other place. Yes, there are still scorpions, centipedes, and tarantulas. I once stepped on a scorpion in my bathroom and had excruciating pain for four hours. The next day at work my leg felt numb. When my wife's sister's husband visited us here one time, he said: "Why do people live here?" I suppose it is a good thing that men desire different habitats, or we would all be crowded into one space.

Dissatisfaction with the rationing system and the environmental conditions at San Carlos resulted in the murder of the army officer in charge at San Carlos, Lieutenant Jacob Almy, in May 1873. The San Carlos agent, Charles Larrabee, had heard of a plan of the Yavapai Chief Chuntz to kill him and as many whites as they could, then to flee to the mountains. It was in the attempted arrest of members of the Yavapai band that Lieutenant Almy was shot, first in his abdomen and then through the head. General Crook was outraged at the murder of Almy and planned an offensive to track down those responsible.

The following September, Capitan Chiquito enlisted as an army scout at San Carlos, possibly as part of General Crook's campaign to bring in the criminals, Chuntz, Cochinay, and Cha-deisa—dead or alive.[4] Although some historical accounts report that Capitan Chiquito was sent to Yuma Territorial Prison at this time for harboring murderers and trading stolen horses with the Zuni, they mistake him for the Hualapai chief, Little Captain.[5]

General Crook appointed Major George Randall as the San Carlos agent in January 1874. One of Randall's first actions was to arrest Eskiminzin and confine him in the guardhouse at San Carlos on New Year's Day 1874. General Crook had always disliked Eskiminzin and agreed with Randall's action. Yet Eskiminzin managed to escape the San Carlos guardhouse a couple of days later, and he and numerous members of his band fled to the wilderness again. Capitan Chiquito remained as a scout at San Carlos until January 31, when Chuntz and Cochinay killed two freighters near San Carlos who refused to give them whiskey. Many Apaches fled the reservation at this time, fearing that they would be punished for this incident. I can only speculate why Capitan Chiquito would desert the army and flee San Carlos at this time. Maybe he was pursuing his old enemies Chuntz and Cochinay, as enlistment records show him deserting on the very day of this incident.[6] Eskiminzin and some of his band surrendered late in April 1874 at San Carlos, yet Capitan Chiquito had not yet returned to the reservation. On June 6, 1874, the Fifth Cavalry detachment and Apache scouts attacked Chiquito and Eskinela's bands in the Santa Teresa Mountains, near Mount Turnbull, killing three men and capturing thirteen women and children.[7]

Capitan Chiquito remained a fugitive until the following August, when he turned himself in at San Carlos. The *Nevada State Journal* wrote:

> Advices from San Carlos say Capitan Chiquito with the last remnants of struggling bands of hostile Apaches surrendered at that place on [August] the 17th. He had fifteen bucks [Apache warriors] with him.[8]

Yet Capitan Chiquito was fortunate. A week before his surrender a new agent had arrived at San Carlos, who would befriend him and change his view of the world forever. His name was John Philip Clum. John Clum was a divinity student who graduated from Rutgers College in New Brunswick, New Jersey. He had once wanted to become a parson in the Dutch Reformed Church. Yet he decided to join the Army Signal Service, and he went west to be stationed at the city of Santa Fe as a weatherman. The Dutch Reformed Church was the denomination responsible for finding a man to serve as agent at San Carlos. Church officials contacted Rutgers College to see if a recent graduate might be interested in the job of serving as the San Carlos agent, and some of Clum's classmates mentioned that Clum, who was already out west, was an ideal candidate for the job.

In one of his many books on the Old West, Neil Carmony writes:

> Clum's appointment to the San Carlos Reservation was largely due to President Grant's Indian Peace Policy, which enlisted Christian religious organizations to assist the Indian Bureau in finding men of high moral standards for these assignments. The policy was based upon recommendations to Grant by a group of Quakers who had embarked on a crusade to solve the Indian problem and the bloodshed that was a daily occurrence on the western frontier. The outline of the plan was as follows: 1) Settle the nomadic tribes on reservations and teach how to be self-sufficient farmers. 2) Introduce the Indians to Christianity and thus elevate them spiritually and cleanse them of their barbaric habits. 3) As Indian-White hostilities subside (and they will when the Indians become Christianized farmers), reduce the role of the military on the Western reservations.[9]

The Apache also had many memories of the "barbaric habits" of the Americans. Did this Quaker vision of the Apache future come to pass? Well, in looking at the San Carlos Apache tribe today, I would have to

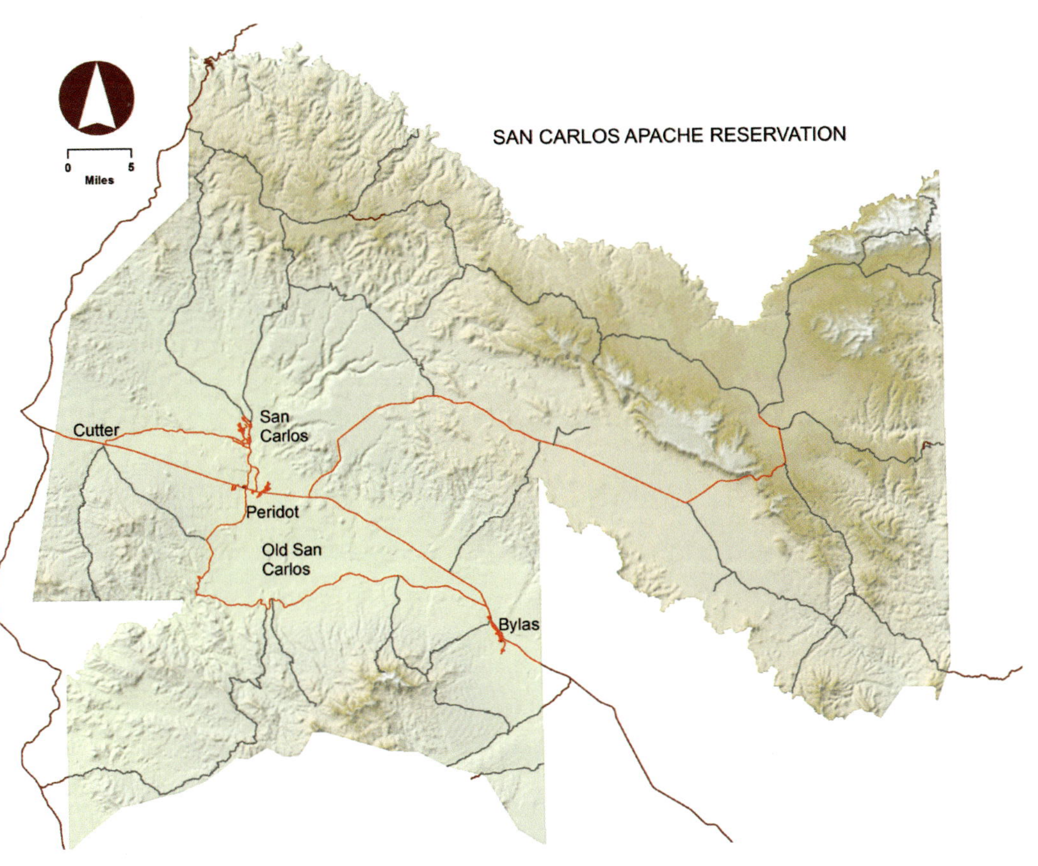

MAP 1. The San Carlos Apache Reservation.
Map by Stevenson Talgo.

FIGURE 1. Velma Bullis, wife of the author, great-granddaughter of
Capitan Chiquito, Chicago, 1971. *Courtesy of her sister, Deana Reed.*

FIGURE 2. Velma Bullis joins a religious order in Chicago, 1973.
Courtesy of her sister, Deana Reed.

FIGURE 3. Lonnie Bullis, grandson of Capitan Chiquito. Globe, Arizona, circa 1972. *Courtesy of his daughter, Deana Reed.*

FIGURE 4. *Coming of the Spaniards.* Drawing by Apache artist Douglas Miles. *Courtesy of Douglas Miles.*

FIGURE 5. Photo of Joyce Tovar, great-great-granddaughter of Capitan Chiquito. She wears the traditional dress worn by a girl for her Sunrise Dance. She is the lady who walked with me on the mesa of the massacre in the introduction of my story. A *gaan* dancer is in the background. *Courtesy of Arizona Highways Magazine and Joyce Tovar.*

FIGURE 6. Shanaya Victor at the top of photo, Janessa Victor on the left, and Lorena Cosen on the right. Lorena is the daughter of my Apache godchild, Melissa Cosen. When Lorena had her Sunrise Dance, her cousin, Shanaya, was her partner. Lorena was the partner for her cousin Janessa at her dance. *Photo by John Hartman.*

FIGURE 7. One of Capitan Chiquito's six wives (probably Mary). Washington, DC, 1876. *Courtesy of the National Anthropological Archives, Smithsonian Institution.*

FIGURE 8. Edward Zinn's painting *Apache Raid*. Zinn witnessed the raid when Aravaipa Apaches attacked wagon trains of the Tully and Ochoa Freight Company. *Courtesy of the Arizona Historical Society, 8181.*

FIGURE 9. Photo of Capitan Chiquito taken on his trip to Washington, DC, with San Carlos agent John Clum, 1876. *Courtesy of the National Anthropological Archives, Smithsonian Institution.*

FIGURE 10. Photo of a well-known landmark on the trail from Old San Carlos to Aravaipa Canyon called White Lady Sitting There. *Courtesy of Phil Hendrick, resident of Aravaipa Canyon.*

FIGURE 11. *Apache Women, Victims of Violence* by
Apache artist Carrie Curley. *Courtesy of Carrie Curley.*

FIGURE 13. The Camp Grant Massacre site in Aravaipa Canyon with the Aravaipa Creek bed in the foreground and Table Mountain in the background. *Photo by John Hartman.*

FIGURE 12. *Facing, Scene of the Camp Grant Massacre, Arizona*, by Vincent Colyer, American, 1825–1888. Date: September 1871. Medium: Watercolor on paper. Dimensions: 10 5/16 × 13 5/16 in. (26.2 × 33.8 cm). The Museum of Fine Arts, Houston, the Bayou Bend Collection, museum purchase funded by M. Robert Dussler, D. Cal McNair, Ray Childress, Scott Schwinger, Dr. C. Thomas Caskey, Malcolm Gillis, Wm. P. O'Connell, Chris Kersey, and Walter E. Johnson in honor of Robert C. McNair and the Houston Texans at "One Great Night in November, 2003." B.2003.8.

FIGURE 14. *Above,* Photo of the monument at Old San Carlos to commemorate all the years the Apache people lived and died in that place. *Photo by John Hartman.*

FIGURE 15. *Facing top,* Photo of the front of the Medal of Honor awarded to Private Chiquito. The medal shows a female allegory of the Union fending off an attacker with serpents in both hands. The two holes at top attached to a medal clasp of an eagle atop a cannon, which connected the ribbon to the medal. *Courtesy of the Arizona Historical Society.*

FIGURE 16. *Facing middle,* Photo of the back of the medal of honor awarded to Private Chiquito. The back of the medal reads: "The Congress to Private Chiquito Indian Scout." This medal was found in an area now known as The Wheatfields north of Globe, Arizona. It was formerly called the "Pinal Maizefields" where the Pinal band grew corn. *Courtesy of the Arizona Historical Society.*

FIGURE 17. *Facing bottom,* Gravesite where the skeletal remains of Yavapai were taken from Skull Cave and buried. *Photo by John Hartman.*

IN REMEMBRANCE OF THE BRAVE YAVAPAI
MEN, WOMEN, AND CHILDREN WHO WERE
MASSACRED AT THE SKELETON CAVE
DECEMBER 1872 BY THE U.S. ARMY

FIGURE 18. Photo of an Apache delegation taken to Washington, DC, in 1876. Front Row (*L to R*): Capitan Chiquito, Chief Eskiminzin, Chief Salgully of the Yavapai, Chief Cassadore. Apache women (*L to R*): Chiquito's wife, Eskiminzin's wife, Cassadore's wife. Back row (*L to R*): Interpreter Merejildo Grijalva, San Carlos agent John Clum. *Courtesy of the National Anthropological Archives, Smithsonian Institution.*

FIGURE 19. Capitan Chiquito and wife (probably Mary). Washington, DC, 1876. *Courtesy of the National Anthropological Archives, Smithsonian Institution.*

FIGURE 20. *Left,* Photo of the Apache Kid taken after his arrest in Globe, Arizona. *Courtesy of the Arizona Historical Society.*

FIGURE 21. *Below,* Gravesite of Sheriff Glenn Reynolds who was killed while taking Apache prisoners to the Yuma Arizona Territorial Prison. *Photo by John Hartman in the Globe City Cemetery, Arizona.*

FIGURE 22. Painting of Capitan Chiquito done in 1898 at Old San Carlos or Aravaipa by Elbridge Ayer Burbank. Gift of Frederick A. Delano, 1899, *Courtesy of the Peabody Museum of Archaeology and Ethnology, Harvard University, PM 99-23-10/54047.*

FIGURE 23. Photo of the Fontaine Sisters at the Walnut Street Theater in Philadelphia. Capitan Chiquito's son, Dajida (Alonzo Speeche), married Vera Pickett who is on the left. This photo was given to me with permission to use by Vera's granddaughters, Delores Lewis and Judy Nolan, who are now deceased. *Courtesy of John Hartman, the author.*

FIGURE 24. Last known photo of Capitan Chiquito (*on the right*). After Lonnie Bullis died, I found this photo under a pile of junk in his shed. The caption on the back read: "This is myself and your Aunt with your grandfather." This was probably written by Lonnie's uncle, Elin Bullis. *Courtesy of John Hartman, the author.*

FIGURE 25. Photo of Capitan Chiquito's son, Alonzo Speeche (Dajida). I found this photo in a collection of Lonnie Bullis's papers after he passed away. Alonzo is making arrows on his farm at Old San Carlos. *Courtesy of John Hartman, the author.*

FIGURE 26. Lonnie Bullis with his two daughters, Velma Bullis on the left and Deana Reed on the right. Taken at San Carlos circa 1983. *Courtesy of Deana Reed.*

FIGURE 27. John Hartman with his wife Velma Bullis. *Author's photo.*

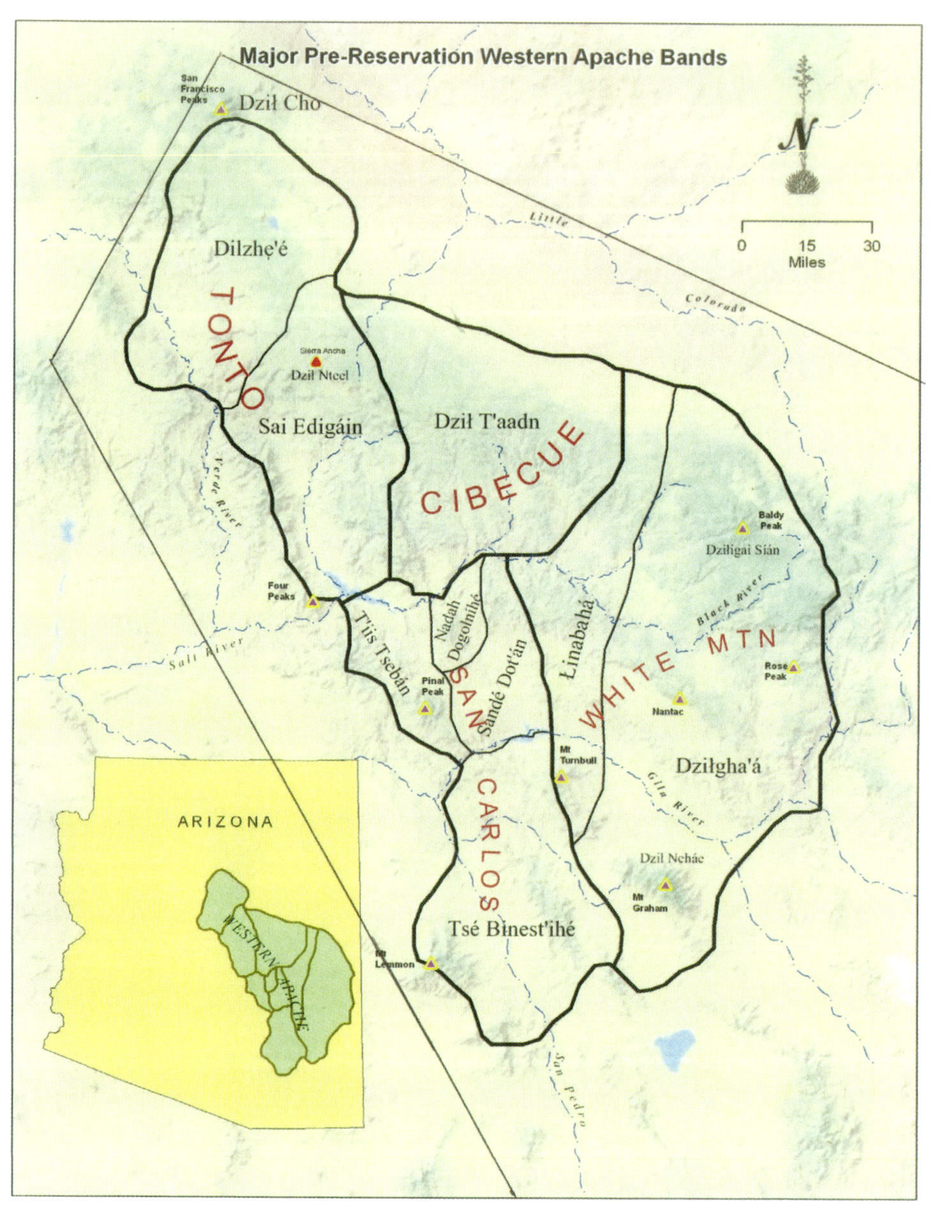

MAP 2. Major Pre-Reservation Western Apache Bands. *Map by Stevenson Talgo.*

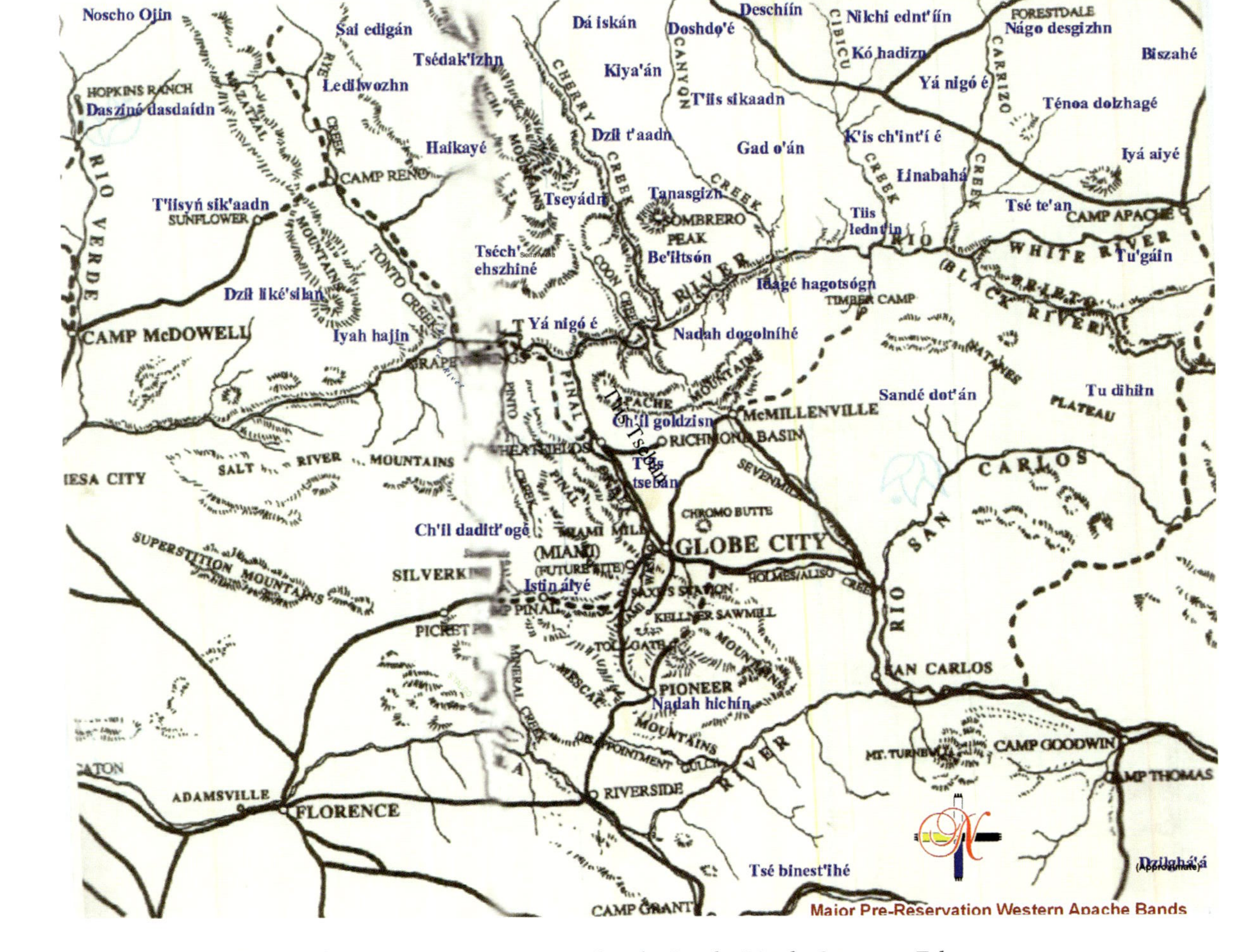

MAP 3. US Army Forts and Pre-Reservation Western Apache Bands. *Map by Stevenson Talgo.*

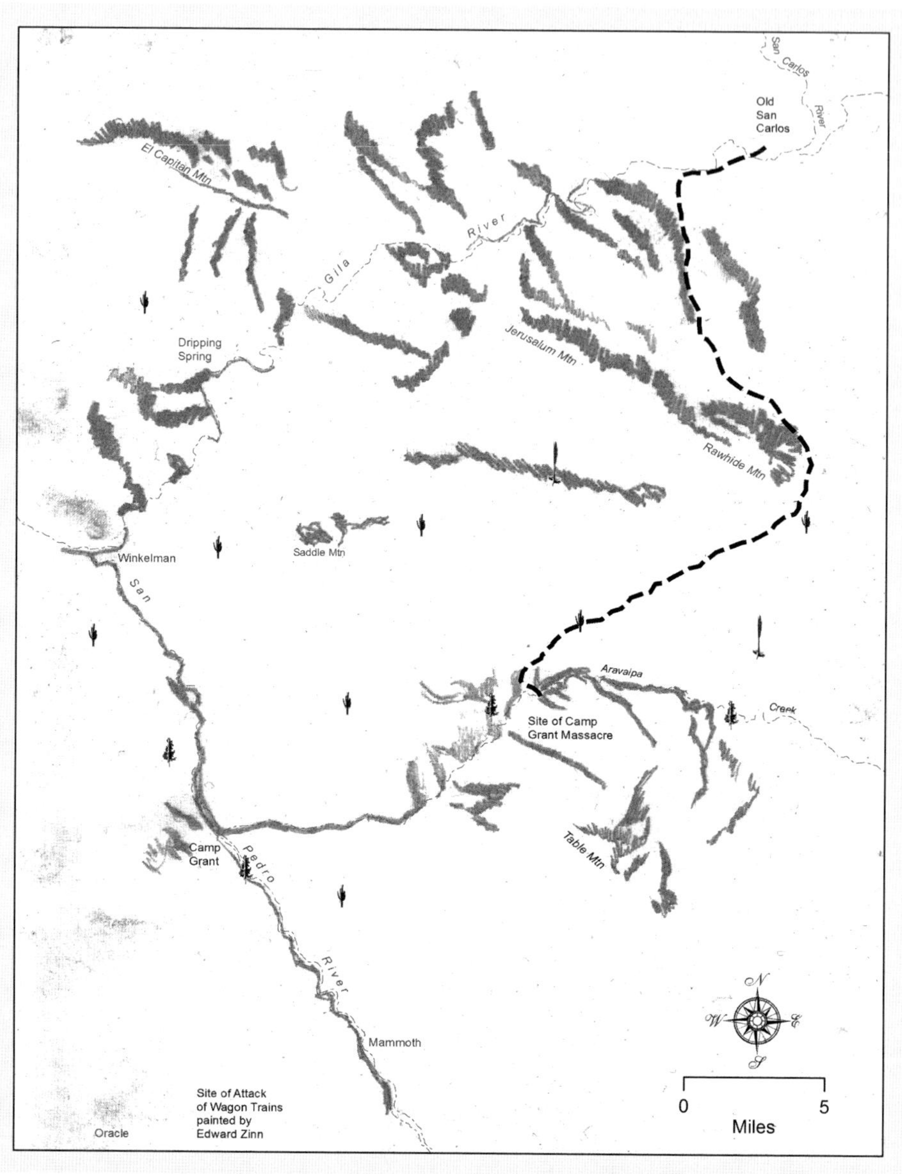

MAP 4. The Trail from Old San Carlos to Aravaipa Canyon with some present-day landmarks. *Map by Stevenson Talgo.*

say that it was pretty naive to think that the majority of the Apaches would be farmers. The Apaches today earn their livelihood in a number of ways, such as casino workers, wildlife protectors and hunters, hospital workers, teachers, law enforcement officers, firefighters, and many other occupations. Some ways that the Quaker policy has come to pass is that the majority of San Carlos Apaches today are Christian, and the only military presence is the San Carlos Veterans Association, which is rightfully proud of its members' service to our country.

Historian James L. Haley writes:

> A new agent, John Philip Clum, arrived at San Carlos on August 8, first greeted by the rotting, gore-clotted heads of Chuntz and his crew. It was a sight to demoralize any man, but it was an especially stark initiation for a twenty-two year old farm boy from New York. Chuntz's final position had been overrun and he and his half dozen supporters were killed. Their heads were brought into San Carlos on July 25, and were displayed for several days on the parade ground.[10]

Clum had Eskiminzin released from his chains at New Fort Grant. Sometime after the massacre near Camp Grant the fort was relocated near Mount Graham in a more defensible location. Eskiminzin became Clum's lifelong friend, and he was very influential in obtaining Apache cooperation with Clum's goals for the reservation. Clum had many goals that he wanted to achieve, yet it seemed his main goal was to give the Apaches the dignity and respect they deserved by demonstrating his trust in them. He established an Apache police force and an Apache Court so that they could have some sovereignty and not have to be guarded by the military. He allowed them to elect their own leaders who would have a say about the goals and future of the tribe. He would allow them to have a gun to hunt with if they checked it out and returned it after hunting. He did have them stop making the intoxicating Apache beverage of *tiswin*, and he enforced this with his Apache police. He helped to decrease their dependence on government rations by giving them the tools to begin planting and harvesting their own crops and fruit trees.

Clum wrote in his diary on March 28, 1875: "Had a trial in the evening and confined two Indians for an attempt to assassinate Capitan Chiquito."[11]

Apparently, these two men were still seeking revenge for Capitan Chiquito's participation in the battle of Skull Cave. In April 1875, Clum granted permission to the bands of Eskiminzin and Capitan Chiquito to move up the San Carlos River about eight miles and create a farm there. These three Apache bands were now cultivating thirty acres and growing beans, corn, squash, and pumpkins.[12]

In May 1876, John Clum received orders to proceed to the Chiricahua Reservation east of Tucson in the Dragoon Mountains and remove the Chiricahua Apache to San Carlos. Clum marched to Tucson with fifty-four Aravaipa and Coyotero men, including Eskiminzin and Capitan Chiquito. This Apache police force was fully armed with government rifles and equipped for war. Some of Tucson's leading businessmen came to Clum and requested an Apache war dance. Clum consulted with the Apaches and found them not only willing but also enthusiastic. In the center of the Old Military Plaza at Tucson a campfire was kindled in the darkness under the light of the full moon. Three thousand spectators surrounded the plaza, as thirty-five Apaches, stripped to their waists with bodies and faces smeared with war paint, performed a wild war dance with blood-curdling war whoops. The audience became terrified at the climax when the Apaches shot off twenty rifles in rapid succession; the audience ran for cover in terror. The show ended with a final salvo from the rifles. Clum called the Apache band to attention and thanked them on behalf of the departed audience and dismissed them. The timid group of Tucson citizens came out of their hiding places when they were assured of their safety, and they congratulated Clum on the very vivid and realistic performance of the Apache scouts.[13]

Clum and his fifty-five Apache scouts next marched east to the reservation of the Chiricahua. The approach of Clum's Apache force and their alkali dust could be easily observed by the Chiricahua lookouts from their posts on the mountain peaks. The war chiefs of the departed Cochise began to encourage the Chiricahua to prepare for battle with this opposing force that they greatly outnumbered. However, the two sons of Cochise, Tahzay and Naiche, opposed the plans of the war chiefs, as they had promised their father on his deathbed to keep the peace treaties he had made with the Americans. In a council of the Chiricahua that night, a fight broke out and Cochise's son, Naiche, shot the war chief, Skinyea, in the forehead, piercing his brain. Cochise's son, Tahzay, then shot another war chief, Pionsenay, in the right shoulder, and Pionsenay fled with some of his followers. The following morning Clum and his scouts arrived in the Chiricahua camp, and Tahzay and Naiche both consented to the removal of their band to the San Carlos Reservation. Four days later, Clum's fifty-five Apache scouts escorted 325 Chiricahua to the San Carlos Reservation.[14]

The amazement and fascination of the people of Tucson with the "Wild Apache Show" in the Tucson Military Plaza gave John Clum an idea. He proposed a trip to the east with a group of Apaches. He would select those chiefs and leaders of the various Apache bands that he felt would be most influential propagandists on their return to Arizona. He would help pay for this trip to the east by having his Apaches perform a "Wild Apache Show" in the various cities they would visit on their way to Washington, DC. John Clum thought that the recent massacre of Custer and his troops by the Sioux would make the easterners all the more eager to see a show put on by a band of wild Apaches.

In the book he wrote about his father's life, Woodworth Clum writes:

> The next step was the selection of the personnel of our party. This was a matter of vital importance, demanding utmost discretion in the selection of each member, with a view to attaining the principal objectives: 1) the influence to be exerted by the members of this party after their return to the reservation; 2) the acting ability required to assure the success of our proposed entertainments; 3) securing a combination that would maintain harmony among themselves; while at the same time endeavoring to avoid any feeling of disappointment that would embitter candidates who were left behind. Our final roster of Apache tourists included Eskiminzin and his wife; Tahzay, chief of the Chiricahuas; Diablo, chief of the Coyoteros, and his son; Salgully, chief of the Yumas (Yavapai); Cassadore and his wife; Captain Jim, of the agency Indian police force, and his wife; Capitan Chiquito, sub-chief of the Pinals, and his wife. Nine athletic young braves and a boy twelve years of age completed the Apache group.[15]

Clum also took with the group Doctor S. B. Chapin, the agency physician, and Merejildo Grijalva, the Mexican man captured by the Apaches as a child, for their interpreter.

Merejildo may have been the one that came to Chiquito one hot summer day and told him that Clum had selected him for a special mission. Perhaps Capitan was told that Clum had chosen him to visit the Great White Chief of the Americans, so that he could impart wisdom to him for his people. Merejildo might have told him that Clum was impressed by his war whoops and dancing for the people of Tucson, and he knows of his influence with the *ndee* (Apache people). I can imagine Chiquito telling Merejildo that he would give this invitation some thought and prayer and give him his answer in the morning. He most likely prayed to Usen and visited the medicine man, Santo, for guidance. Santo perhaps told Capitan of his visit to the East five years ago with the American Nantan (General) Howard, who lost one arm in the war where the Americans were trying to kill each other. Santo may have showed him the "Peace Medal" that the war chief, and now, the "Great White Chief" of the Americans had given him. Capitan Chiquito agreed to go with Clum and the other chiefs. He would take his youngest wife, Mary, and let his other wives stay behind to take care of the children and his crops and fruit trees.

On a warm July morning they left San Carlos; a great crowd of their people gathered to bless them for their journey. They traveled on wagons drawn by horses, and in a week they arrived at Silver City, New Mexico. It took them one full cycle of the moon to reach the place called El Moro in Colorado, where they reached the "road of iron" (*Besh be tin*). Chiquito's wife, Mary, was trembling when they climbed up the great Iron Horse, and she began to weep when the great beast moved forward with great shrieks and bellows. She was not afraid when they crossed the mesas and mountains, but when the great beast began to move, she wept, feeling that she would never see her home again.

On their way, Tahzay, the chief of the Chiricahua and son of Cochise, was boasting that he did not think his father had acted wisely in making peace with the white man. As he saw the vast expanse of land with no white people on it, he felt that they could still defeat these white men from the East. But as they passed through Denver, Kansas City, and climbed up to the great dome of the City Hall at Saint Louis, Tahzay was silent. The young chief was still proud of his people, but he admitted that he now realized how unequal their fight had been.

In the city of Saint Louis, the Apaches were led into a great hall called the Olympic Theater to put on a performance for the white men. They stripped to their waists, painted their bodies with warpaint, and sang Apache songs around the campfire. They were then attacked by the white men: John Clum, the white medicine man Doctor Chapin, and Merejildo the interpreter. There were gunshots and fighting, and the screams of battle, but the white man defeated them in this act. There were paintings behind them showing forests and canyons. Capitan's wife, Mary, came out to mourn for the dead. She lamented and cried, yet the white people thought the whole thing was funny, and they laughed out loud.

In another scene, the Apache attacked and killed the white men. They were told to take scalps. The Apache do not take scalps, but they did this because Clum asked them to, and this is what the crowd expected of them. They performed a war dance, and the crowd seemed somewhat frightened by their war whoops. They did two more performances at the Olympic Theater, yet each night there were fewer and fewer people to see them. Clum said that it had to do with the American war chief, Custer, who had been killed by the Sioux.

When they left Saint Louis, Clum said there would be no more performances. They journeyed to the capital city of the Americans. They saw the great building where the Americans held their councils. They visited the place they call the "White House," and they were told the story of all the great white chiefs who had lived there. They were told the story of a man called Lincoln, who was shot in the head behind this very building at the end of the war where the Americans were killing each other. They were told that Lincoln had been killed eleven years ago, because he gave the black white men their freedom. Perhaps they wondered why Lincoln freed the black white men, yet he allowed his army to hunt the Apaches like animals and take their freedom away.

Capitan Chiquito and the other chiefs met President Grant. Clum probably told the president that these chiefs lost loved ones at the fort that was named after him. They were later shown many great things. They had never been on a boat before, yet they traveled down a river called the Potomac to a place named Mount Vernon. There were many talks with the white men and the white men took many photographs of the Apache, and body measurements. In the great capital city of the Americans called Washington, the chief of the Chiricahua, the son of Cochise, Tahzay died. They knew his death was not a good omen and could bring great tragedy to many. Tahzay had a ghost sickness that perhaps could have been cured by one of their Apache medicine men, and they were sorry that Santo, their medicine man, was not with them. The white medicine man tried very hard to save him, yet Tahzay's lungs gurgled and gurgled, as if he was drowning.

The white men placed Tahzay's body in a box of wood that they lifted onto a wagon drawn by black horses. They buried him in a place where they said that many of their great men were placed beneath the earth with markers of white stone (the Congressional Cemetery). A priest in ceremonial robes may have explained to them that the Apache God,

Usen, was the same God that they honored and worshiped. Yet I don't think the Apaches would understand why they carried their tortured God, Jesus, on a pole nailed to a tree. They saw this tortured God, Jesus, often when they raided the homes and the missions of Mexico. The Mexicans seem to delight in the torture of their God. Jesus looked as if they had dragged him through a field of cactus, bleeding from every place on his body. Around his head was a ring of cactus that caused his blood to stream down his face.

On their journey back home on the Iron Horse, they stopped in the city called Philadelphia. They were having a great celebration there, because it had been one hundred years since the Americans had fought and won their freedom from a great nation across a large sea of water to the east. The things that they saw there must have made them dizzy. In a building so huge that they feared it might fall down on them, they saw machines of medal that did things that were hard to understand. It must have made them feel very small. I believe that Eskiminzin, Capitan Chiquito, and the other chiefs may have had somewhat of a conversion experience here and realized that it would be foolish to try to fight these Americans anymore. These Apache men never fought the Americans again. Had Tahzay not died, perhaps the Geronimo campaign would never have taken place. Instead, Tahzay's brother, Naiche, would become chief and ride with Geronimo on his path of war.

Clum traveled with them on the Iron Horse back to Colorado, then Merejildo traveled with them on wagons back to San Carlos. Clum had returned east, because he had finally found a wife. He told them that he would return to San Carlos with his new wife.[16] Perhaps Capitan Chiquito and Eskiminzin laughed that a man who seemed to have so much power could only find one wife.

10

Clum and Apache Scouts Capture Geronimo and Clum's Resignation as San Carlos Agent

WHEN CLUM ARRIVED BACK in San Carlos in January 1877, he took six of the chiefs who had made the trip east with him on a reservation tour to meet with each of the five major bands now located there, which numbered 4,500. His goodwill tour went well until they came to the rancheria of the Chiricahua. With the death of Tahzay, Cochise's other son, Naiche, was now chief of the Chiricahua Apaches. Naiche was quite enraged with Clum for the death of his brother, who he felt had been poisoned or killed by evil spirits of the white man. Eskiminzin explained to Naiche the details of Tahzay's illness, his diligent caretaking by the white medicine men, and his elaborate and honorable burial in a place called the Congressional Cemetery, where many great white chiefs were laid to rest. Naiche seemed content with the explanation and said that the words of Eskiminzin had softened the pain in his heart.

When Clum and his Apache scouts brought the Chiricahua band to the San Carlos Reservation, Geronimo and his band of warriors did not come in. Geronimo was not a chief, but through his mystical powers of clairvoyance he became a respected and charismatic war chief. Geronimo and his warriors were making frequent raids through southwestern New Mexico, and the army troops had been unable to capture him. The Arizona Territorial governor, Anson P. K. Safford, requested of Clum sixty of his San Carlos Apache police to serve as a territorial militia to protect the people of Tucson and the surrounding ranches. Clum marched sixty of his Apache police to the town of Tucson and placed his chief of police, Captain Clay Beaufort, in charge of them. They were an Arizona National Guard and could not pursue Geronimo into Mexico or New Mexico. Geronimo and his band were discovered to be making their headquarters and drawing rations at the United States Government Agency at Ojo Caliente, New Mexico, near the present city of Truth or Consequences. When this news arrived at the War Department in Washington, DC, the following telegram was sent to John Clum:

> *Washington, DC*
> *March 20, 1877*
> *Agent Clum, San Carlos, Arizona*
>
> If practical, take your Indian Police and arrest renegade Indians at Ojo Caliente, New Mexico. Seize stolen horses in their possession; restore property to rightful owners. Remove renegades to San Carlos and hold them in confinement for murder and robbery. Call on military aid, if needed.
>
> *(signed) Smith, Commissioner*

The agency physician, Dr. S. B. Chapin, who had traveled to Washington, DC, with Clum and the Apaches, tried to dissuade Clum from what he said was a suicidal mission. Chapin pointed out that Ojo Caliente was two hundred miles beyond the Arizona border and that eleven troops of United States cavalry had been unable to find or trap Geronimo. Yet Clum gave the following telegram to his courier:

> *Safford, Gov. of Arizona*
> *Tucson*
>
> Am ordered to take Apache police and capture Geronimo at Ojo Caliente, New Mexico. Will need my company of Apaches now in service of Arizona territory. Request they be returned immediately to my jurisdiction.

The following day Clum received a telegram from the governor approving his request. Then Clum wired Captain Beauford, in command of the sixty men of the Apache Militia Company, to march at once to Silver City, New Mexico, and await his arrival. Soon afterward, Clum left San Carlos and began the four-hundred-mile march to Silver City with forty dependable and well-trained Apache police on foot.[1]

The distance from San Carlos to Silver City would not be four hundred miles with today's highway system, but Clum chose first to go to Fort Bowie for some reason, and who knows what route he may have taken.

Capitan Chiquito and Eskiminzin were no doubt pleased that they were going on this adventure and that they would be issued government rifles. Their friend Hautushnehay, who had traveled with them to Washington, DC, was also one of the forty Apache police officers who would go. My belief is that Clum called Hautushnehay, Sneezer, because his name sounded like someone sneezing to him. The descendants of Hautushnehay on the reservation today are the Sneezy family. Even Cochise's son, Naiche, would go on this mission. The Apaches in this group knew every hill and creek and canyon of the Chiricahua country, and they were ready for a new adventure.

If Geronimo had seen the wonderful things that they had seen in the great American cities, he would know his foolishness in not cooperating with the Americans. They told Clum that they did not need his maps, as long as the sun shone and the stars appeared in the sky. Four hundred miles even on foot was no challenge to the Apache, and they must have made fun of Clum, who thought that twenty-five miles a day would be sufficient. They told Clum that they would do forty miles a day and enjoy it. It must have given them the sense of freedom and joy that they once knew before the Americans placed them in their concentration camp. One evening after covering only thirty miles, which Clum thought a great deed, they did a war dance for two hours to show Clum that he and his men were not getting enough exercise.

As they came near Fort Bowie, they told Clum that there was a great sandstorm coming. It had perhaps been conjured up by Geronimo, whose powers they had witnessed before. Clum was doubtful, yet he respected their abilities to read the signs of nature. The sandstorm came at night and raged for almost two days. It tore the paint off all the wagons and left their eyes and the eyes of the mules bloodshot. The sun rose in a brown haze and shone with a weird light. They repaired their moccasins, for every Apache knew how to make his own. They ate mostly beans and flour and pork. But Clum brought some shotguns, so they also ate desert quail, jackrabbits, and wild turkey. None of them doubted that they would capture or kill Geronimo.

At Fort Bayard, New Mexico, Clum received a telegram that three army troops of horsemen would meet them at Ojo Caliente. The Apaches did not like this news that Clum gave to them. The Apache did not have to discuss this, as the white men do. Around their campfire they looked at one another and exchanged their feelings without words. Then they had Ezkiminzin talk to Clum in words that he could understand, and he told Clum that they did not want the white soldiers to help them to get Geronimo. Geronimo is Apache as they are Apache. They knew how Geronimo's warriors fight and they knew that white soldiers do not know how to fight Apaches. However, Clum explained to them that Geronimo had at least one hundred fighting men and that they needed the army to help capture him. Yet Usen smiled on the Apache, and the horse soldiers would arrive too late.

They met Captain Beauford with his militia of sixty Apaches at Silver City. Clum had obtained some horses for them in this place and twenty-two rode to where Clum was to meet the army major at Ojo Caliente. Captain Beauford and the other eighty Apaches were to wait about half-way between Silver City and Ojo Caliente at a spring twenty miles away. It must have been good to be on a horse again and to feel like a free man and not confined to the reservation. When they arrived at Ojo Caliente, Clum was given a telegram from the army major who said he could not be here for two days. They learned from one of their Apache scouts that Geronimo with one hundred followers was camped about three miles from the agency, and that he had come to the agency that very day for rations. Geronimo must surely have known of their presence at Ojo Caliente now, but he probably thought their twenty-two mounted police was their entire force.

Clum had a plan that he called the "Trojan Horse." He sent word to Captain Beauford to bring his Apache reserves in the cover of darkness with utmost caution and silence. The captain arrived before the sun came up and Clum had all eighty Apaches hide themselves in a large commissary building, each with thirty rounds of ammunition and his gun loaded. Then Clum sent a messenger to the camp of Geronimo to tell him and the other chiefs that he desired to have a talk with them. The Apaches with Clum were ordered not to shoot unless Clum or the captain gave the signal, or if Clum and the captain began shooting, or unless Geronimo's warriors began shooting.

There was a large parade ground formed by the agency building on the west side, the commissary building on the south side, and a deep ravine to the north and east. Clum and six of the Apache police waited at the agency building to the west. Eight spread out on a skirmish line on the north side near the ravine, and another eight formed a skirmish line opposite them to the south in front of the commissary building, where the eighty Apache reserves waited.

The medicine man, Geronimo, and one hundred of his followers marched into the plaza as the sun rose above the mountains. Perhaps Geronimo had been drinking Mexican tequila, as his powers failed him. He did not sense the trap that they had set for him. He walked in with his subchiefs, Gordo, Ponce, and Francisco. With his armed warriors behind him, they walked proudly and defiantly up to Clum at the agency building. Clum was a clever man and brave. He told Geronimo that he had broken his promise to him to come in to San Carlos, and that he was here to take him back to San Carlos. He told Geronimo that he did not want any trouble, and if he would cooperate with him that no harm would come to him or his people. Geronimo told him that they were not going back to San Carlos, and if he was not careful Clum's body and the bodies of his Apache police would stay here at Ojo Caliente to make food for coyotes.

Then Clum gave the signal, raising his left hand and touching the brim of his sombrero. Instantly, the commissary doors swung open and, like a swarm of hornets, eighty armed Apache warriors flew out of their nest with loaded rifles. They took their positions on the south and east side of the parade grounds, rifles leveled, ready for instant action. Geronimo and his entire band were completely surrounded between two crossfires. Clum was watching Geronimo's thumb on his rifle to see if he would cock it. For a moment it looked like he would fight, yet all of their rifles were pointed at him, and he decided not to die that day. Geronimo told Clum that they had been on the warpath for a long time and they were tired, and he was ready now to have a big smoke, and talk. Clum said that a big talk could not happen until they put away their firearms, and he ordered Geronimo to have his men lay their guns on the ground.

Clum took Geronimo's rifle himself, and he later wrote that he had never seen anyone look at him with such hatred in his eyes, as Geronimo did. They gathered up the rifles of Geronimo's men on the parade ground, and the captain put a guard around the weapons in the commissary. This rifle that John Clum took from Geronimo is now on display at the Arizona Historical Museum in Tucson.

There was no bloodshed that day, and the Apache were happy that they had captured Geronimo and his band, yet they probably regretted that they had not been able to fire the rifles that they had been given.[2]

Clum had Geronimo and his six subchief's taken to the agency blacksmith shop, and, in full view of Geronimo's band, had iron shackles and chains fastened to the ankles of each of them. Shortly after this, Victorio, the chief of the Warm Springs Apache, came into the agency to speak with Clum. Seeing shackles on Geronimo and his subchiefs, Victorio was enraged. Clum explained to Victorio that Geronimo was being punished for the murder of two teamsters and other raids that had killed men, women, and children. Clum explained to Victorio that Geronimo had fifty stolen head of cattle in his encampment three miles from the agency. With Clum's powers of persuasion, Victorio agreed to go with Clum and his whole band to San Carlos, at a distance of four hundred miles. Clum had sent Captain Beauford with seventy-five mounted Apache police to apprehend other Apache raiders who were reported to be committing depredations to the south. This left Clum with only twenty-five Apache police to guard the 453 Apache that made up the bands of Geronimo and Victorio. They began their march back to San Carlos on May 1, 1877, reluctantly accepting the assistance of twelve US troopers under the command of Lieutenant Hugo. The long march through the desert was completed on May 20, 1877, and nineteen prisoners, including Geronimo and his shackled chiefs, were locked in the San Carlos Agency guardhouse. Clum added Victorio to his council of Apache judges, and peace and industry resumed their dominance. Yet Clum became enraged when a company of soldiers was sent to San Carlos to help manage the Apaches and perform inspections. Clum was unable to convince the War Department or the commissioner of Indian Affairs to remove the soldiers, which he was convinced would only cause resentment among the Apache.[3]

Frustrated with the military, who would not allow Clum to manage the San Carlos Reservation as he saw fit, Clum turned in his resignation, and at the end of July 1877, he said his farewells to the San Carlos Agency. Eskiminzin and Capitan Chiquito told Clum that they could not stay at San Carlos, as they saw troubles for themselves if the army tried to manage things. Perhaps with Clum's assistance, they were allowed to settle at the southernmost boundary of the reservation. Eskiminzin began to grow his crops along the San Pedro River near

Old Camp Grant. Capitan Chiquito returned to the site of the massacre on Aravaipa Creek, and with his six wives began to plant an orchard, seeded fields of corn, and dug irrigation ditches to make them flourish. Clum told them that perhaps he could better help them as a private citizen and said he would always be their champion in the newspaper that he intended to establish.

John Clum's son, Woodworth Clum, wrote the book *Apache Agent*, and in it he remarks:

> Within two weeks after John Clum had resigned as Agent, in July, 1877, Geronimo had been released from the guardhouse, his ankle-irons removed; he had been given the freedom of the reservation, supplied with new blankets and food for himself and his families. Upon whose orders this murderer of at least one hundred men, women, and children was turned loose has been a mystery for more than half a century. Geronimo should have been hanged not later than August, 1877. His record for murder and robbery was common knowledge. Clum had risked his life and the lives of his loyal police in effecting Geronimo's capture; had marched on foot eight hundred desert miles to do the job. If Geronimo had been promptly hanged, that great serio-comedy, known as the "Geronimo Campaign" (1881 to 1886), would have been avoided; five hundred human lives and twelve million American dollars would not have been sacrificed, and the United States Army would have been spared its most inglorious record of Indian warfare.[4]

Clum first went to Tucson, where he bought the *Arizona Citizen*, a weekly newspaper, changing it to a daily paper. However, a booming mining town, with the ominous name of "Tombstone," soon drew him to that place. Tombstone received its name from a prospector named Ed Schieffelin, who found a large vein of silver there. The story goes that Al Sieber, the chief of the Apache scouts, told Ed that if he kept wandering in the desert by himself looking for a mine, that the Apaches would someday find him and kill him and all we will find of you is your tombstone. So Ed thought this would be an appropriate name for his booming mining town. Within six months, ten thousand men built a city on a lonely desert mountain that had only been inhabited by coyotes and creatures of the wild shortly before.[5]

In Tombstone John Clum became the editor of a newspaper that he called the *Tombstone Epitaph*, as he said that "no tombstone is complete without its epitaph."[6]

There was once a contest to name the local newspaper of the San Carlos Apache tribe with a $500 reward for the winner. Contestants were also supposed to choose a logo for the newspaper. My wife chose the name "The Cacti Times." She was a good artist and she spent quite a bit of time drawing some varieties of cactus with a desert background. I told her that I did not think Apaches would relate much to that name. I knew that the hummingbird is thought by many Apaches to be a messenger from the spirit world. I copied two hummingbirds off the internet and submitted the name "The Apache Messenger." Velma was not very happy with me when I won the contest, so I bought her a new vacuum cleaner with the prize money.

John Clum became a friend of the Earp brothers, and he was the mayor of Tombstone when Wyatt, his brothers, and Doc Holiday shot down three men at the O.K. Corral. The town of Tombstone receives thousands of visitors each year who want to see the O.K. Corral where three men were gunned down. Yet not many know or care about a lonely mesa near Old Camp Grant, where 120 Apache women and children were murdered.

Capitan Chiquito Returns to Aravaipa Creek

WITH THE HOPE OF being left in peace, Capitan Chiquito with his six wives and children returned to the place of his birth on Aravaipa Creek. Two of his wives were Mohave, three of them were Apache, and one a Mexican captive. Their names were Josepha (probably the Mexican captive), Carrie Lane, Goodegula (my wife Velma's great-grandmother), Rough Mohave, Laura, and Mary. Mary was the wife he had captured from the Mohave when she was a child. The land around Aravaipa Creek was a beautiful and lush place, plentiful with herbs, agave, and berries for their sustenance. However, Chiquito and his wives would labor to turn this place into a Garden of Eden. With irrigation ditches from the creek, they established an orchard of fruit trees and planted crops of grain. The painful memories of this place may have been purged by purification rituals by the medicine man.

Grenville Goodwin is apparently referring to Capitan Chiquito in the following passage on plural marriages, when he refers to the marriage with six women: "Of the twelve polygynous marriages recorded from the period before 1880, in all but two the husbands are known to have been wealthy and influential men, and in five of them they were true chiefs. Of these marriages, eight were with two women, two with three women, one with four women, and one with six women. In the marriage with six women, the first was of clan 20 (slender peak standing up people), the second of the same clan, and later on, becoming very wealthy, the man married the other four, respectively, of the Pinal Band, San Carlos Band, Chiricahua Apache, and one a Mexican captive."[1] One of Capitan Chiquito's wives was a Mexican captive, yet another was a Mohave captive. Chiquito also had one wife named Rough Mohave, who no doubt was of the Mohave tribe. Whoever gave Goodwin the information on Chiquito's wives did not have all their facts straight.

In 2008 two books were published about the Aravaipa Apache: Karl Jacoby's *Shadows at Dawn* and Ian Record's *Big Sycamore Stands Alone*. The history professor at the San Carlos high school began to use these books to teach his Apache students about their own Apache history. The knowledge of their Apache history for most students was limited to the warrior Geronimo, who most students took great pride in. In the spring the students would then take field trips to Aravaipa Canyon, which sometimes included the company of the authors of these two books. They were also accompanied by the tribal botanist Seth Pilsk, who would educate the students on medicinal and edible plants in Aravaipa Canyon. Seth assisted the Apache elders Vincent Randall and Jeanette Cassa with their book *Western Apache Trees and Shrubs*. This fascinating book has beautiful photos of the plant life in traditional Apache lands with the English, botanical, and Apache name of each plant.

Ian Record writes: "Not long after returning to their homeland, Hashke Bahnzin [Eskiminzin] and Chiquito had become prosperous commercial farmers, transporting their often substantial crop surpluses to sell in nearby towns such as Winkleman, Mammoth, and Dudleyville. Three years after establishing his ranch, Hashke Bahnzin reported that he had become self-sustaining and no longer needed agency rations. He declared, 'I bought all my family clothing and supplies with the money I made.'"[2]

Anne Price, the daughter of Chief Diablo, was most likely referring to Capitan Chiquito in the following passage:

> Anne Price also related how her mother, on a visit to the encampment of a man with six wives, each living in a different wickiup, asked some of the women in fun, "What kind of people are all these living here?" She spoke of them as if they were a whole local group or band. "Oh, they are all kinds mixed together; na dots usn (slender peak standing up) clan, San Carlos Band, Chiricahua people, every kind," the woman answered

her in a similar tone. The old man, the husband of these women, was sometimes joked by other people. He used to decorate his face with brown mescal juice, and when he did this people would say, "Well, you must be out after another woman again," to which he would good-naturedly answer, "The time was when I visited all six wikiups every night, but now I only visit four. I am getting old. I'm sort of going downhill now. I'm staying with my Chiricahua wife. She takes good care of me and makes all my clothes. The others won't do that for me." Because each wife had a separate wickiup of her own, and what was really only one family looked like a whole family cluster, a man with several wives was sometimes jokingly alluded to as "The chief of his wives," or "His people (following) are his wives."[3]

Historian Karl Jacoby writes:

Capitan Chiquito, who was, as one of his descendants, Wallace Johnson, recalled, "rich in wives," followed a similar pattern, taking out an allotment in Aravaipa Canyon with his six wives, each of whom inhabited her own gowah (wickiup). Capitan Chiquito's camp became the nucleus around which other Ndee (Apache People) may establish farm sites of their own. Remembered one of the people, James Nolin, "Chiquito was recognized as sort of chief of the Indians on this Aravaipa Canyon near San Pedro. [T]his camp extends along the canyon several miles, his own family camp was just part of this big camp. Like Hashkee ba nzin, Capitan Chiquito became a successful commercial farmer renowned for his delicious peaches and figs. In many cases, the proximity of their new homes to the massacre site was striking: while Hashkee ba nzin's homestead and several of the other Nnee families were located a few miles below Blue Water Pool (old Camp Grant), Capitan Chiquito's farm embraced the lands around Big Sycamore Stands There (the massacre site). Other people, while not taking out homesteads, made annual trips to the canyon to gather acorns, saguaro fruit, and other wild foodstuffs. How the Nnee reconciled such behavior with their cultural inhibitions about coming in contact with the dead is unclear. But the People had previously returned to Aravaipa after the killings of their kinfolk there in 1832 and 1863, despite what observers at the time reported to be a great number of skeletons scattered across the canyon floor. It may be that the Aravaipa's ecological riches or the tug of other, happier memories outweighed the concerns about disturbing Nnee remains. Or that once ceremonially purified—a custom that usually involved the use of tobacco or corn pollen to ward off the spirits of the deceased—the canyon's bones and grave sites no longer posed as great a peril as they might have otherwise.[4]

I have heard so many Apache ghost stories that I once considered writing a book on this topic alone. Many of the stories were told to me by the Apache ambulance drivers and emergency medical technicians, who seemed particularly adept at spotting ghosts along the highway at night. There are places on the reservation that always gave me goosebumps when I drove at night, such as the "Never Again Bridge" that I crossed on my way to work. I always had the distinct impression that someone was sitting in the back seat of my car, as I approached the bridge and crossed over it. It was called the "Never Again Bridge" because each time they rebuilt it, as the flooding San Carlos River took it out, they would say that they would never again have to rebuild it.

Another whole genre of stories I often heard were the "little people" and "Bigfoot" stories. One well-known hunting guide on the reservation told me that he was hunting one day and had the sensation that someone was watching him on the ridge behind him. He turned around to see a small, bearded man looking down at him. The little humanoid ran down the ridge away from him. As he told me the story I could see the hairs on his arms stand up as he remembered this creepy story. I would sometimes spot coatimundi as I hiked on the reservation; they looked kind of like a cross between a monkey and a raccoon. The guide who told me this story knew every creature on the reservation, and he would not mistake a coatimundi for a little man.

Most of the reservation is uninhabited with many places to explore. When I would camp at night it was pitch black and deeply silent. There was something otherworldly about it. The veil between this world and the next seemed quite thin.

About 1880 Capitan Chiquito established a friendship with his old nemesis, Jesus Elias of Tucson, who had led the raid of 1871 where two of Chiquito's wives had perished. He visited the home of Jesus Elias several times with his wife, probably Goodegula, with whom he had one daughter and three sons. His wife Josepha was a Mexican woman, so it is unlikely that he visited with her.[5]

According to Jesus's daughter, Alvina Rosenda:

After the Indians stopped fighting Capitan Chiquito and my father became very good friends indeed. After a time he married again, an Indian woman about thirty and very good-looking. He brought her to see us and father bought some bright colored cloth and mother and her sister made the bride some new dresses. Father also gave her a good horse, a saddle, and all sorts of fine trappings. Later, when a little girl was born to Capitan Chiquito, he brought her to the house and wanted mother to keep her and bring her up like the white people, but mother felt that the responsibility was too great. Mrs. Capitan liked me very much and took my measurements so as to make me a beaded bracelet and necklace. We gave her our address but for some reason we never got the things. The last time Capitan came to see father he brought some presents; a cane covered with blue and white beads and a doll made of buckskin. But when he got to Tucson Mr. Angulo told him that father was dead and that the family had moved out to the Mission. We did not see him that time nor did we ever see him again.[6]

After Karl Jacoby wrote his book *Shadows at Dawn*, he invited Velma and me to Tucson to have dinner with three of Juan Elias's great-grandchildren: Ramon, Juan, and Yvette. The great-grandchildren of these two rival Apache and Mexican American families were able to establish a friendship and share stories about their lives and the lives of their ancestors.

In August 1881, an uprising of Apaches on the White Mountain reservation would temporarily expel Capitan Chiquito and his wives from their Garden of Eden and force them to return to San Carlos. The medicine man, Nock-ay-det-klinne, who had been a scout at the battle of Skull Cave against the Yavapai, was doing a Ghost Dance at Cibecue. He was saying that his dance would cause the dead Apache chiefs to rise again and that all the white men would be forced to leave Apache land. His following became so great that the army determined to arrest him, and on August 28, 1881, two companies of cavalry under Colonel Eugene Carr left Fort Apache to carry this out. However, many of the Apache scouts turned on the soldiers as they tried to arrest Nock-ay-det-kinne, and the battle that ensued resulted in the death of Captain Hentig and several of the soldiers.[7] During the battle, Nock-ay-det-kinne was shot and killed by the soldiers, and from his neck was taken one of President Grant's peace medals, which reads: "On Earth Peace, Goodwill Toward Men. 1871."[8] There is no evidence that Nock-ay-det-klinne had ever been to Washington, DC, and this medal was likely given to him by Santo, Pedro, or some of the other Apache who had accompanied General Howard to Washington in 1871.

The Apache scout who shot the captain off of his horse was called Dandy Jim. Dandy Jim was likely the only recipient of a congressional Medal of Honor who would subsequently be hung for desertion and the murder of an army officer. Dandy Jim had been awarded his medal for gallantry in the battle of Skull Cave against the Yavapai, and he was later hung at New Fort Grant, along with two other rebellious Apache scouts, Dead Shot and Skippy.

In the uprising that took place after the death of the medicine man, Fort Apache was attacked, and many soldiers and civilians were killed by the Apache throughout the reservation area. Troops were called in from army posts within Arizona and outside of Arizona to help put down the rebellion. General Wilcox issued a field order "giving the Indians throughout the reservation five days notice that he was establishing 'a peace line' around the Agency and Subagency effective September 21st, and that any Indians found outside of its limits would be considered hostile, 'except scouts, runners, and others in the military service, and the friendly Indians of Pedro's band near Fort Apache.'"[9]

So, at this time Capitan Chiquito and other Aravaipa families returned to San Carlos with many other Apache who lived outside of the "peace line." One hundred and fifty Chiricahua warriors led by Chief Juh fled the reservation, passing through Aravaipa Canyon on their way to Mexico.[10]

In September 1882 General Crook assumed command of the Department of Arizona and Philip Wilcox became the new San Carlos Apache agent. In his book on the battle of Cibecue Creek, Charles Collins writes: "At about that time Crook asked Agent Wilcox to let the agency Indians live wherever they wished within the boundaries of the reservation. Wilcox agreed to do so under conditions that those who moved away from the agency became self-supporting as soon as possible. He also agreed to give them rations and supplies until they could gather their first crops the following fall; however, they had to pack them out to their camps."[11]

In August 1883, Capitan Chiquito enlisted as a scout in Company F of the US Army.[12] Many of the Apache scouts were off the reservation pursuing Geronimo and other Chiricahua bands. Capitan, who was now about sixty, was possibly induced to enlist to beef up the home guard, or as an observer in Aravaipa Canyon, which was often used as a corridor by the Chiricahua to and from Mexico.

In the spring of 1884 Lieutenant Charles Elliott reports: "On the Aravaipa were several small camps, one of them the home of Capitan Chiquito, with his six lusty young wives."[13]

I don't believe that any of Chiquito's wives were young at this time and there is no evidence that they were lusty. It was for security and sustenance that Apache women accepted a plural marriage.

Most likely referring to Capitan Chiquito, Lieutenant Elliott continues:

> The effort was also to uplift the Indians in their domestic life and to discourage the custom of having more than one wife, six being the greatest number known. A very thrifty old chief, with an eye to cultivating a good farm with labor entirely under his control, took six young wives, all good workers, and the result was so satisfactory that it was impossible to induce him to reduce his family.[14]

Geronimo and other Chiricahua Apache bands had returned to the reservation in February 1884. Again, the army was lenient with him and gave him lands for his people and government rations. However, his spirit was discontent and would not let him rest. He made another escape from the reservation in May 1885 with many Chiricahua warriors.

In July 1884 Capitan Chiquito had been transferred to Company B under Lieutenant Britton Davis.[15] Perhaps he was transferred to this company because of his knowledge of Mexico, as Lieutenant Davis was preparing to pursue Geronimo into Mexico. It was time for another adventure for Capitan.

Chiquito may have been sad about leaving his wives and children and the fruit trees he had planted on the Aravaipa, yet he had to trust that his wives would take care of them for him. At the same time, he was probably excited about seeing some of his old haunts in Mexico again. He may have recalled his adventures in Mexico and the brave things that he and his warriors had done there. The warpath was a special spiritual walk, and it brought you power when you were successful. He may have remembered the respect and awe that his warriors had of him, because of the wisdom and insight of his plans for harvesting the Mexican cattle and horses.

They set out from the San Carlos Reservation in May 1885 under the young Lieutenant Davis. He probably knew they would never capture that medicine man, Geronimo, under the command of this young army officer, but he may have been glad to be among his fellow scouts with a rifle in his hand again. Geronimo would never again be so careless as to fall to the trickery of the "Trojan Horse" that Clum had carried out. They crossed into Mexico with 130 Apache scouts and about forty of the army men on horses. They once encountered the camp of Chief Chihuahua, but the Chiricahua fled when they saw them coming from afar. However, they were kind enough to leave them their breakfast of a fat cow that they had cooked. They had several small battles with Apache stragglers here and there, yet Geronimo was clever enough not to take the force on directly. A group of them once followed the trail of three of the Chiricahua and surprised their camp. The men had escaped, but they killed one woman and captured fifteen women and children prisoners.

In one Mexican town they came on called Nacori, there were 313 Mexicans living there, but of these only fifteen were adult males. Every family had lost one or more members at the hands of the Apache. They marched for three months through the mountains and desert valleys of Mexico until their rations and supplies were exhausted. Geronimo had gone east toward the town of Chihuahua, hoping to raid some unsuspecting village.

They then headed toward El Paso in Texas. Lieutenant Davis went before them to assure their passage at the border. At first the border guards did not believe he was an American army officer, being out of uniform, dirty, and with a four-month growth of beard on his face. Yet Davis told them with anger that soon a large group of hungry Apache warriors under his command would arrive, and they would cross the border, whether the border guards liked it or not. When the border officer saw the Apaches approaching, he crossed himself and said, "Válgame Dios" (God bless me). They returned to San Carlos on the Iron Horse.[16]

Capitan Chiquito had been a US Army scout from August 1883 to August 1885.[17] When he returned to San Carlos, he probably wanted nothing more to do with the army and did not reenlist. He returned to his wives, his children, and his farm on the Aravaipa. He had ten acres of fruit trees and crops growing there.[18]

His homecoming to Aravaipa was a sad one. Many of his fruit trees had withered in the summer heat, and four of his wives had left him. Only Josepha and Mary remained. Goodegula even left behind their son, Dajida (my wife Velma's grandfather) for Mary and Josepha to look after. He was only a boy of three. Capitan went to work with Mary and Josepha to save the trees that he could.[19]

That year a lieutenant named Watson came to Capitan's land and set up stones on four corners. He explained to him that the 160 acres between the stones would be his, if he could farm this place for twenty-five years.[20] Perhaps it was strange to Capitan how the white man could claim a piece of land that the Usen had given to all. But if this would mean that they would never take the place of his birth away from him again, he may have been content with that. They also gave Eskiminzin, a parcel of land on the San Pedro and sent papers to the US Land Office in Tucson.

The medicine man and warrior, Geronimo, finally surrendered himself to General Nelson Miles in September 1886. Miles had sent away all of his family as prisoners to a land far away called Florida. Capitan Chiquito thought, perhaps, he would have peace now, or maybe his visionary "star power" saw storm clouds gathering.

Trouble's Name Is The Apache Kid

ABOUT 1860 THERE WAS a boy born into Capitan Chiquito's Aravaipa band, the Tsejine, who came to be known as "the Kid" and, in later years, "the Apache Kid." He was a member of the SA (San Carlos Apache) band. At this time all Apaches on the San Carlos Reservation were forced to wear a brass tag around their neck when they wanted to draw a weekly ration of food and supplies. Capitan Chiquito was SA1, being chief, and the number on each of his band members began with SA.

The Kid was a boy of eleven at the time of the infamous Camp Grant Massacre, which must surely have left a deep impression on him. Kid was later to become a scout in the US Army, and due to the leadership abilities he displayed and his courage on the battlefield, he would eventually become First Sergeant Kid. He was known to possess "running power," and one of his Apache comrades once stated that he could outrun a horse. He also possessed extraordinary eyesight, and it was said that he could see things at a great distance that officers and enlisted men could not even distinguish with field glasses.[1]

On May 3, 1887, an earthquake measuring 7.5 on the Richter scale rocked Arizona and Sonora and is thought to have been the greatest geological event in that area in 10,000 years. The epicenter of this earthquake was near the Sonoran town of Bavispe, only about fifty miles south of where Geronimo had surrendered to General Miles just eight months before. Perhaps some thought that Geronimo conjured up this event, while sulking in his prison cell in Florida, as a last act of revenge on the Mexicans he hated so much, ever since they killed his first wife and children. A church collapsed in the town of Bavispe, killing seventy people. The quake made a crack in the bell tower at San Xavier del Bac in Tucson and is said to have caused the church bells to ring in Mexico City almost a thousand miles away. In Aravaipa Canyon some of the mountain peaks were lowered by several hundred feet as the earth shook violently, and miners in the nearby town of Mammoth ran to the surface as the mine belched dust and rumbled angrily.[2]

This earthquake caused great fear among the Indian peoples, some of whom believed that the world would soon come to an end. A medicine man named E-cha-waw-ma-hoo began a Ghost Dance at a place called Coyote Hole, about halfway between San Carlos and the town of Globe. He performed certain rituals and said that God would soon come in person to restore to the red man the land, and that the white people would vanish and would never come again. It was a time of great excitement and anxiety and over one thousand people were gathering at Coyote Hole.[3]

It is not known whether the earthquake or the chaotic atmosphere generated by the Ghost Dance had anything to do with the decisions and the actions of Sergeant Kid at this time, yet the events that followed are somewhat baffling. In the same month of May in which the earthquake occurred, Sergeant Kid and several other Apache scouts deserted their post at San Carlos and went on a three-day drinking spree with other members of their band. In the previous December, Kid's grandfather had been murdered and the man he felt responsible was named Rip. He decided to avenge the death of his grandfather and headed to Aravaipa Canyon with some other scouts to carry out this purpose. Upon reaching the camp of Capitan Chiquito's SA band, one of Rip's wives saw Kid and knew what he was up to. She ran down to the creek to warn Rip, who tried sneaking up behind the camp, but Kid found him and killed him with one shot through his heart. Having revenged the murder of his grandfather, Kid and his four fellow scouts returned to San Carlos.[4]

Historian Clare McKanna states:

> In effect Kid had administered the retributive law followed by most Apaches and formerly accepted by the federal government. Despite his

belief that under Apache tradition he was right to kill Rip, Kid and his fellow scouts still felt it necessary to submit themselves to Army authority. No doubt Kid must have been somewhat apprehensive when he turned himself in, but apparently he believed that Captain Pierce, his military commander, would be fair in administering punishment for leaving his post.[5]

Kid and his fellow scouts rode up to the tent of the chief of scouts, Al Sieber, and were ordered to put down their rifles and ammunition belts. They complied, but they were accompanied by several armed members of their band. When the Mexican interpreter told them that they would likely be sent to Florida, where Geronimo was being held, several shots rang out; the chief of scouts was shot in the left ankle, crippling him for life. The Apache scouts then ran for their freedom on foot. They were joined by twelve other Apaches, who were apparently bored with reservation life and looking for adventure. As the group headed south and passed through Aravaipa Canyon, Capitan Chiquito was probably already concerned that he might somehow be held responsible for this murder that took place near his home.

After the Apache fugitives passed through Aravaipa, they split into two groups. One group of seven led by the Kid, and the other group of ten by Gonshayee. While stealing horses, Gonshayee's group killed a man near Mammoth on the San Pedro River. Kid's group also killed a man near Crittenden, while trying to steal supplies.

The Ghost Dance at Coyote Hole was attracting hundreds of Apaches and was a worrisome reminder of a similar dance and medicine man that had caused the Apache uprising at Cibecue about seven years earlier. General Nelson Miles came to San Carlos from headquarters to take charge of the situation personally. The Apache scouts were growing tired after being pursued for three weeks by army troops. They sent word to General Miles, saying that they wished to come in, apparently feeling that he would treat them fairly.

McKanna remarks:

> By voluntarily returning, Kid had agreed to submit to military law and accept his punishment. Kid believed that he had not done much harm and that he would be treated fairly by General Miles. The aftermath of Kid's court-martial suggests that the general felt that since Kid had honored their agreement and returned of his own volition he deserved a fair hearing with appropriate punishment.[6]

General Miles ordered a court-martial for mutiny and desertion for the five Apache scouts. The other raiders would be tried in the territorial courts. The five scouts were found guilty and sentenced to death by a firing squad. General Miles appealed this decision and a later judgment ordered them to Alcatraz Island for hard labor for the rest of their lives. They left for Alcatraz in January 1888.[7]

Capitan Chiquito may have been sad, but probably relieved, when Kid was sent away to Alcatraz. He had known Kid since his childhood. Chiquito probably hoped that his life would be peaceful now. Yet a few months later, people from Tucson raided the rancheria of his close friend Eskiminzin. Eskiminzin's ranch was only about six miles from Chiquito's rancheria. Lieutenant Watson from San Carlos came to Eskiminzin and told him that settlers who wanted his land planned to kill him and that he should come at once to San Carlos for army protection.

Eskiminzin left his wife and children behind, thinking that he was the only one in danger. Just one day after he left, a vigilante force descended on his ranch and laid waste to his whole settlement, destroying the homes and all of the crops. The vigilantes stole livestock and terrorized the ones that had remained behind.

> Ian Record quotes Eskiminzin in regard to this assault:
>
> Watson came to my ranch and gave me a paper from Pierce, the agent, and told me I had better go to San Carlos Reservation; that citizens would kill me if I did not; that there were about 150 citizens coming with pistols. They came the next day after I left my ranch, and they shot at my women, putting bullet holes through their skirts, and drove them off. They took 513 sacks of corn, wheat and barley, destroyed 523 pumpkins, and took away 32 head of cattle. I took my horses, wagons and harness with me to San Carlos.[8]

Chiquito knew that he too could be a target of such a raid, but he did not want to return to San Carlos. He had labored too long to create his Garden of Eden. Yet it was not the people of Tucson that would bring Chiquito trouble, but one of his own kinsman.

To the great joy and surprise of Kid and his fellow scouts, and to the anger and bewilderment of the people of the Arizona Territory, Kid and his comrades were pardoned after serving only ten months of their life sentence at Alcatraz. After reviewing their case, the judge advocate decided that there was prejudice among the officers serving on the jury and that the crime the scouts had committed was not serious enough to warrant such long prison terms. The secretary of war agreed and ordered their release on October 29, 1888.[9]

Because the Kid had received a dishonorable discharge, he was no longer able to work as an army scout. He settled on a small farm with his wife about six miles below San Carlos on the Gila River. He was seldom seen, except when he came into San Carlos on ration day. Although Kid was not the one who had shot Al Sieber in the ankle, he was thought to be the ringleader of the gang, and many were still angered by his release by federal authorities. One year after his release from Alcatraz, Kid was re-arrested by the Gila County sheriff and his deputy. On October 29, 1889, he was brought to trial at the Gila County Courthouse in Globe, along with nine other Apache men who were being tried for various crimes. In a trial that lasted but one day, Kid was found guilty of assaulting Al Sieber and was sentenced to seven years in the Yuma territorial prison. On November 1, the Kid and seven other Apache prisoners were loaded into a stagecoach at Globe for the two-day trip to Casa Grande where they would then take the train to Yuma.

After the first day's journey they spent the night at the Riverside stage station. The next morning the shackled and handcuffed Apache prisoners were loaded again into the stagecoach for the journey to Casa Grande. It was raining as they left the station, and four miles down the road they came to the steep uphill climb known as the Kelvin Grade. Knowing that the horses would not be able to pull the coach up this hill on the wet road, Sheriff Glenn Reynolds ordered six of the prisoners out of the coach. The Kid was considered too dangerous to be let outside the coach, so he was left inside shackled to another prisoner. The stagecoach went ahead of them, and Sheriff Reynolds walked in front of the six prisoners, who were handcuffed in pairs with another guard armed with a rifle walking behind them. The sheriff carried a double-barreled shotgun, but his Colt .45 pistol was under his buttoned heavy overcoat. As the stagecoach pulled out of view, the two prisoners who walked behind the sheriff suddenly jumped on him, knocking him to the ground and holding him between them, as they wrestled for his shotgun. At this same moment the two prisoners in the rear knocked the guard to the ground, seized his gun, and shot him through the heart. They next turned the rifle on the sheriff, still struggling for his life between the other two prisoners, and sent a bullet through his neck, killing him instantly. Taking the manacle keys from the body of the sheriff, the prisoners freed themselves and Bach-e-on-al, who had shot the sheriff and the guard, ran swiftly to the stagecoach. He took aim at the coach driver and shot him through the neck. After freeing the Kid and the other prisoner in the stagecoach, the Apache fugitives fled in all directions.[10]

The direction that Kid took was to Aravaipa Canyon and the camp of Capitan Chiquito.[11]

Ever since the Kid's escape, he was always thereafter referred to as the "Apache Kid" in newspaper accounts. The events that transpired in Aravaipa Canyon on his arrival are somewhat sketchy, but the Apache Kid's life, thereafter, would always be a mystery. According to Chiquito's wife, Josepha, the friends of Chiquito killed her brother, Augustine Ruiz, and ran her off when her husband left with the Apache Kid. In another part of Josepha's testimony, she said it was Chiquito's brother who killed her brother.[12]

It is unclear why Chiquito left Aravaipa with the Apache Kid, and it is unclear how close he was to the Apache Kid. In newspaper accounts thereafter, Chiquito stated that he was forced to go with the Apache Kid, presumably because of his knowledge of Mexico from his many raids into that country. The Apache Kid had some knowledge of Mexico from his journeys there during the Geronimo campaign, but his knowledge of Mexico was not as extensive as that of Chiquito. It is difficult to believe that Chiquito would by choice want to leave the land he had worked so hard to cultivate, and to endanger his possession of it, by this risky venture. Whether Chiquito was taken by the Apache Kid by force or whether he went willingly is unknown, yet the newspaper accounts always assumed that Capitan Chiquito went willingly.

It is likely that Capitan Chiquito got wind of his impending arrest sometime before March 1890 and fled with his wife, Mary, and son, Dajida, with the Apache Kid, rather than face imprisonment. On March 10, 1890, the San Carlos Indian agent, Captain John Bullis, had seventy-five friends and relatives of the Apache Kid in Aravaipa Canyon arrested. He had them sent to Fort Union, New Mexico, under guard with the accusation that they were giving supplies and aid to the Apache Kid and his renegades. Twelve children from this band were sent to the Ramona Industrial School in Santa Fe, New Mexico.[13]

Historian Douglas Meed writes of some of Capitan Chiquito's adventures with the Apache Kid:

In a series of skirmishes with troopers of the Fourth US Cavalry during the summer of 1890, the Kid's band was badly shot up. But in August he and a companion named Chiquito, ambushed, robbed, and killed three Americans in the lonely Big Hatchet country in the southwest "boot heel" area of New Mexico. On August 16, 1890, Alfred Williams of Hachita, Carl Elmer of Deming, and Peter Riggs of Elmerys Spring, were killed at Hachita, about fifty miles southwest of Lordsburg, New Mexico.[14]

This incident took place on August 16, 1890, according to Earle Forrest and Edwin Hill's story of the Apache Kid. They state:

Captain Keyes left Lordsburg immediately with fifteen troopers in pursuit of the hostiles. Near the scene of the murder they discovered the trail of two Indians and one led horse. General Miles reported that these Indians were evidently Apache Kid and his companion Chiquito. When they near[ed] the Mexican border the soldiers found where the three other Indians had joined this pair. Captain Keyes followed the band across the line into Mexico, but the trail was finally obliterated by rain, and the troops were forced to turn back.[15]

The following month the *Arizona Daily Citizen* printed this article in its September 15, 1890, edition:

THE KID
His Horse Captured North East of Mount Turnbull Mountain.
Capt. Chiquito Gives Up.
He is tired of Renegade Life and Wants to Quit.
Kid's Squaw [*sic*] Comes into San Carlos and Tells of the Renegade's Worn Out Condition.
This morning General Royal A. Johnson received a letter from his ranch partner Mr. E. A. Stratton which is reproduced verbatim below.
It appears that Capt. Chiquito is a father-in-law of the Kid and has lived for many years at the mouth of Aravaipa Canyon on a small ranch. Capt. Chiquito was considered a peaceful Indian and has been well spoken of by the settlers of the San Pedro until the killing of Sheriff Reynolds in the spring at Globe by the Kid, when the old man joined the renegades band. His squaw stated that he was taken at night by force by the Kid. Complaints were made before his joining the Kid's band that he was furnishing these parties with ammunition and scouts set out from San Carlos to effect his arrest, but the bird had flown. The letter reads as follows:

Mammoth, A. T.,

September 10th, General Royal A. Johnson,

Tucson, A. T.

DEAR FRIEND: John Forrest the white man who married the Apache squaw [widow of Pat Cashen] who lives on the Aravaipa came into this place this morning and reported to me that Capt. Chiquito came to his house night before last and requested Forrest to inform the authorities at San Carlos that he was there and wanted to give himself up.

Yours respectfully, E. G. Stratton

Following on this matter Capt. J. Fowler, Troop I, 2nd Cavalry was in the city this morning having just returned from a hot pursuit of the Kid. The Capt. said to a Citizen representative: Two parties from Ft. Grant, one from Ft. Thomas and four from San Carlos started after the Kid on the report of a squaw who came to San Carlos on about the 2nd, who said she was the Kid's squaw and had left him the previous night at 11 o'clock at a point near Black Rock, South East corner of Turnbull mountain. Also that she and the Kid had separated from a party en route from Mexico four nights before consisting of Kid, herself, Capt. Chiquito, wife and boy. That Capt. Chiquito said he and his party were going to try to work back to his ranch in the mouth of the Aravaipa. That he wouldn't stay longer with Kid and for him to kill no more whitemen. She said that Kid had told her that the troops were after him and that he couldn't take care of her, but to take his pony Buckskin and go in. She stated that she was captured by Kid from Guadalupe's band on the Cibecue and that she was a White Mountain Apache and wanted to return to her people. The squaw stated that the Kid was in reduced circumstances, riding a bay pony, without saddle, and had but one carbine and one belt of ammunition. The troops came up with the Kid's pony at the second canyon north east of Turnbull. The rider had vamoosed for the hills.[16]

The wife with Chiquito must have been his Mohave wife Mary (since all his other wives had fled). The boy with them was most likely my wife Velma's grandfather, Dajida (who was about eight at the time). The Apache Kid is still a legend among the San Carlos Apaches today. His clan, the Tsejine, were somewhat stigmatized because of the troubles that the Kid brought to the whole Apache tribe. I once gave a framed photo of the Apache Kid to the day-care center across from the hospital where I worked; the day care was called *Apache Kid.*

13

The Imprisonment and Exile of Capitan Chiquito

THE MURDER OF THE Gila County sheriff and his deputy would send ripples down through the generations that would change the destiny of my wife's family and that of many other Aravaipa families, such as the Kindelays, the Curleys, and the descendants of Eskiminzin. Within a year of their escape, five of the Apache fugitives would be killed in gun battles with their pursuers, and two of them captured and sent to Yuma prison, where they both died four years later of tuberculosis. Although he had been seen numerous times, the Apache Kid was never killed or captured, and thus he became a legend. With a $5,000 reward offered for the Kid "Dead or Alive," he was pursued by the military, Apache scouts, and bounty hunters without success.[1]

Historian Douglas Meed states:

One who should have known the Kid's fate was Sonora's chief of Rurales, Colonel Emilio Kosterlitzky, an old Apache fighter, who at the turn-of-the-century said that the Kid was still holed up in a rancheria near the Continental Divide on the Chihuahua-Sonora border. In later years, older Apaches at San Carlos said that the Kid was making stealthy visits to relatives and friends there well into the 1920s.[2]

Most San Carlos Apaches today believe that he lived out his life in the Sierra Madre Mountains of Mexico. There is an Apache song performed at some social gatherings that tells of the Kid looking down with sadness on San Carlos from the top of Cold Water Springs Peak, north of San Carlos, and wishing that he could give up his fugitive life and live among his people again. The song goes partially as follows:

> Anah, hiyu, Anah, hiyu
> Oh, they say I was involved
> Yes, they say I was involved
> But, I was not
> Now they want to send me far away
> Yes, they want to send me far away.

Charlie Victor relates that his father, Glenn Victor, said that the Apache Kid last visited San Carlos in 1924 and that he had a family in Mexico. It is said that on this visit he gave out gold coins to some of his relatives and clothing to the children.[3]

After his surrender, Capitan Chiquito for the first time in his life faced the humiliation of leg irons and imprisonment at the Old San Carlos guardhouse. His wife and children were confined at Fort Wingate, New Mexico (near Gallup). After spending nine months in the Old San Carlos guardhouse, Capitan was then sent to Fort Union, New Mexico (near Las Vegas,), where his wife, Mary, and children were also to be transferred.

In May 1891 the acting Indian agent for San Carlos, Captain John Bullis, sent the following two dispatches:

Assistant Adjutant General
Department of Arizona
Los Angeles, California

(Through the Office of the Commanding Officer,
U.S Troops, San Carlos, A.T.)

Request that Captain Chi-qui-to who was a renegade Apache, now held at my request by the Commanding Officer, be sent to Fort Union, New Mexico, to be held there in confinement with other Indians from here.

J. L. Bullis, Acting Indian Agent

And in another letter to the same office, Bullis writes:

Request that the five Indians held in confinement here, friends of the renegade Kid, with their families numbering about ten, also the wife of Captain Chiquito, who is now held at Fort Wingate, be sent there for confinement. Total number about sixteen.

Bullis, Acting Ind. Agent[4]

After a period of confinement at Fort Union, New Mexico, the families of Capitan Chiquito, Eskiminzin, Kindelay, Curley, and other Aravaipa families (a total of forty-six individuals) were placed on a train and sent to the Mount Vernon Barracks, near Mobile, Alabama, sometime in 1892.

The military employed the same strategy that they used to force Geronimo's surrender in the hopes of having the Apache Kid turn himself in, or, at least, that he not be assisted by his family to hide and have supplies brought to him. Since they were unable to capture the Apache Kid, they sent his mother, his wife and children, and all his close relatives away. At the Mount Vernon Barracks, Capitan Chiquito and his kin would join Geronimo, Naiche, and 341 other Chiricahua Apaches who had been transferred there from Florida.

Southwestern scholar H. Henrietta Stockel writes of the conditions at Mount Vernon on the arrival of the Aravaipa Apaches:

Owing to the number of Indians sent here from the west during the year [46] and to the fact that the village was constructed for only those here at the time, there is not sufficient room to house all in the new village; consequently there are five families living in the log huts of the old village, exposed to all the dangers of its unsanitary condition and location.[5]

Of her visit to Mount Vernon in the 1990s, Henrietta Stockel writes:

The hot and steamy climate is extremely uncomfortable for someone accustomed to the high desert living in the Southwest. Even the act of breathing seems different here—more obvious, harder, wetter. It is decidedly darker than it was on the road just a few minutes ago. Mosquitoes appear and quickly perch on bare faces, arms, and legs. The welts they raise are world class. Ignoring the impediments, however, there is an almost overwhelming sense of being in this place, but it feels sad and heavy. Only the dead weight of sorrow is left. And it is practically palpable.[6]

In August 1893, Geronimo wrote a letter from Mount Vernon Barracks to Lieutenant Hugh Scott saying, "Young men, women, and children all want to get away from here—it is too hot and wet—too many of us die here."[7]

The death rate was high at Mount Vernon due to diseases such as malaria, pneumonia, and tuberculosis. It is estimated that over 250 Apaches are buried at Mount Vernon in unmarked graves.[8]

Eugene Chihuahua, son of Chief Chihuahua, stated:

> We had thought that anything would be better than Fort Marion with its rain, mosquitoes, and malaria, but we were to find out that it was good in comparison with Mt. Vernon Barracks. We didn't know what misery was until they dumped us in those swamps. . . . It rained nearly all the time. . . . The mosquitoes almost ate us alive. . . . Babies died from their bites. . . . Our people got the shaking sickness. . . . We burned one minute and froze the next. . . . No pile of blankets would keep us warm. . . . We chilled and shook.[9]

With or without their parent's consent, many Apache children were taken away and sent to various boarding schools. Many of the schools had a high rate of tuberculosis, including the Carlisle Indian School in Carlisle, Pennsylvania. The superintendent of Carlisle was Captain Richard Pratt, who would send sick and dying children back home to their parents for their final days. Often the parents had not seen their child for years and they were reunited with them only to watch them suffer and die.

Capitan Chiquito and his wife, Mary, had at least three of their sons taken from them and sent away to boarding schools.

One of their sons was sent home after becoming ill and died shortly after he returned.

My wife Velma's grandfather Dajida was sent to the Grand Junction Indian School in Colorado, where his long hair was cut, his moccasins taken away, and he was given a school uniform. Even his name, Dajida, was taken from him and he was given the name of Alonzo Speeche.[10]

Capitan Chiquito had another son whose Apache name is unknown. He was possibly also sent to Grand Junction and given the name of John Bullis. The younger sons, Rex and Elin, were probably confined at Mount Vernon with Chiquito and Mary, as they were known as Rex Chiquito and Elin Chiquito.

The *Arizona Silver Belt* of Globe, Arizona, had this to say about the death rate in some of the Indian boarding schools in its October 27, 1894, edition:

> Indians Returning Home. Three years ago one hundred and five Apache Indians left the San Carlos Reservation, thus carrying out the government's policy of segregation and isolation from tribal relations thereby instilling into the mind of the Aborigine the higher principle of our civilization. How far has it succeeded? On the 15th [of this month] there arrived at Safford in charge of Henry Wigmann thirty-eight out of the formerly one hundred and five, the rest are lying beneath the sod at Genoa, Nebraska. This fearful role mortality is a sad commentary upon the government's policy of educating the Indian. Pneumonia and consumption were the weapons used to civilize the sad remnant of this fierce race, many of the children return only to find the paternal camp fire gone out, father and mother having departed to the happy hunting ground. Three years at the Genoa Industrial school has been more fatal to these people than the deadly aim of the Pioneer.[11]

In the Indian school at Grand Junction, Colorado, where Capitan Chiquito's son, Dajida (now Alonzo Speeche), was sent, the children were not allowed to speak their language, sing their songs, or to perform any of their traditional tribal dances or ceremonies. A Navajo woman had this to say about her son at Grand Junction:

> They fall one by one to the ground until finally the wind sweeps them all away and they are gone forever. . . . The parents of those children who were taken away are crying for them. I had a boy who was taken from this school [Fort Defiance] to Grand Junction. The tears come to our eyes whenever we think of them. I do not know whether my boy is alive or not.[12]

Dajida (Alonzo Speeche) spent six years of his life at the Grand Junction Indian School, and at the age of sixteen he was sent to the Carlisle Indian School in Pennsylvania to begin the eighth grade. Some of the children at Grand Junction missed their relatives and former way of life so much that they would run away from the school and try to find their way home.

In the Annual Report of the Commissioner of Indian Affairs for 1892 we read:

> The mystery surrounding several runaways from Grand Junction would never be solved. Originally seven boys ran off. The superintendent apparently did all that could be done, sending trackers into the mountains

and telegraphing civil authorities along expected escape routes in hope of intercepting them. Two of the boys made it safely to their homes. A third joined the Army. As for the remaining four, officials never could account for their whereabouts. It was thought that Arthur Ducat, one of the two who made it home, might shed some light on the mystery, but all efforts to extract information from him elicited nothing helpful. Several statements made by him had been followed up and found not to contain one iota of truth. The missing four were never heard from again.[13]

One unhappy boy at Grand Junction, who had been given the name of Rip Van Winkle by some superintendent with a strange sense of humor, wrote the following letter to the agent at Fort Defiance:

February 20, 1894
Dear Sir:

I am going to write to you this morning I don't like stay here. I want go home. I have stayed here over four years and half pretty nearly 5 years. I want to write the Commissioner for me so I can go home. I want see my folks. I had been here a long enough I think so I wish you to write to the Commissioner for me. I think you know my grandfather. I cannot spell his [name] but I can tell you where he lives. I think you will know him. He lives at foot of the mountains on the road that goes to the sawmill. I wish you would tell I said. If does not who I am tell to ask George Bancroft. He can tell him who I am. Tell him I am not feeling well and want to come home I want to see my grandfather pretty bad. He is getting old and nobody to do his work I think. I think you would not know what tribe I am from. I am from the Navajo tribe. I am getting tired of this place and want to come home this summer if you will be kind enough to write to Washington for me. If you will I'll be obliged most all of the Navajo boys want to go home to see their people. They are anxious to go home. That is all for this time. Hoping to hear from you soon.
From yours Truly,

Rip Van Winkle[14]

Although the US government had always intended to keep the Apache prisoners of war east of the Mississippi River, after years of bureaucratic haggling it was finally decided that Fort Sill in Oklahoma Territory would be a healthier location for them. The citizens of Mobile objected to the move. H. Henrietta Stockel writes:

The Indians were a popular tourist attraction, and their presence added to the dollars flowing into the local economy. Even the newspaper was worried—about the lack of interesting stories about the prisoners that would result. But being transferred was fine with the Apaches.[15]

Official orders were drawn up by the army for the transfer on September 18, 1894. The news made many people nervous and angry. Including the people of Globe, Arizona, which is near the San Carlos Apache Reservation. In the *Arizona Silver Belt* of September 1, 1894, the Globe newspaper wrote:

> A Chicago dispatch gives tongue to the damnable action of Congress regarding the return of the infamous Chiricahua Indians from Alabama to San Carlos, Arizona. They are first to be put on probation at Fort Sill Oklahoma, and if after a brief period there, they commit no murders, they will be conducted by military escort to their old home on the Gila River near the San Carlos Agency. A visitation of cholera would be preferable to the return of the Chiricahua.[16]

A list was prepared with information about some of the prisoners as part of the closeout procedures. Of some of the Aravaipa Apache prisoners, the following was written:

> Chiquito—Very industrious and faithful, age 70; Eskiminzin—Character excellent, a farmer; Kindelay—a hard worker, age 40; Curly—Very industrious, age 38; Stovepipe—Inclined to be idle, age 35; Nock-e-lah—Industrious, age 40; Bechole—Inclined to be idle, age 35; Tille-chille—Very industrious, age 40.[17]

The Chiricahua Apaches boarded the train for Oklahoma on October 4, 1894, yet the Aravaipa Apache were left behind as military and government officials debated what to do with them. John Clum had made a visit to Mount Vernon in January 1894 and was surprised to find his friends Ezkiminzin and Chiquito there, who had accompanied him to Washington, DC, eighteen years previously. Clum began a letter writing campaign to senior military and government officials to gain freedom for the Aravaipa prisoners. Yet there were some, such as General Nelson Miles, who strongly opposed the idea.

Lieutenant Hugh Lenox Scott relates in his memoirs:

> Returning to General Miles' camp, I recommended that Geronimo, Naiche, and their people be sent to Fort Sill, and Eskiminzin and his people be sent home to Arizona. General Miles flushed up at hearing

the recommendation in the case of Eskiminzin and became quite angry. He declared that Eskiminzin should never again set foot on the soil of Arizona as long as he, Miles, was alive because Eskiminzin had buried a white man up to his neck in an ant-hill. I reminded the general that this had been wiped out by the lapse of twenty-five years, and that he himself had condoned many acts of savagery in the case of other tribes; why single out Eskiminzin who had lived an extremely good life for many years?[18]

Ian Record remarks:

Whether because of Clum's efforts or in response to news of Apache Kid's apparent death, the Office of Indian Affairs acquiesced, ordering their release later that year. In order to protect them from possible reprisals by Arizona citizens, the US Army secretly transported them under heavy security back to San Carlos.[19]

Alberta Kindelay of San Carlos relates that her father, William Kindelay, was born on the train on the ride home from Alabama and they named him after the conductor of the train, who had assisted them with the childbirth. William would later be a medicine man at San Carlos.[20]

Lieutenant Hugh Scott reports of the Aravaipa Apaches return to Old San Carlos:

Several years after, a troop of the First Cavalry that had escorted Eskiminzin from the railroad to their agency came from Arizona to Fort Sill, and Lieutenant Osborne told us that those Apaches ran far ahead of the wagons, with the tears of joy streaming down their faces as they recognized the landmarks in their old country. The agent established them on their reservation, where they proved to be the most industrious, well behaved and progressive people he had, a notable example to the others.[21]

Capitan Chiquito and Mary were overjoyed to be back at San Carlos, yet they missed their home on Aravaipa Creek, which they had been exiled from during the four years of their imprisonment. They also missed their son, Dajida, who was undergoing a harsh indoctrination at the Grand Junction Indian School in Colorado. They would not see him again for many years.

"He Once Rendered Valuable Service to the Government"

CAPITAN CHIQUITO AND MARY returned to San Carlos with the other Aravaipa families. They had been away from their home on Aravaipa Creek for five years. He had spent approximately one year with the Apache Kid before his four years of imprisonment, which was first in the San Carlos guardhouse, then at Fort Union, New Mexico, and finally at Mount Vernon, Alabama.

After farming at San Carlos for about two years, Capitan Chiquito petitioned the Indian agent, Captain Meyers, to be allowed to return to his land on Aravaipa Creek. Captain Meyers allowed him to do so, but he warned Chiquito that his land most likely was being occupied by other citizens. Sometime in 1897 Chiquito, Mary, and some other Aravaipa families returned to their homeland. Eskiminzin had died not too long after returning to San Carlos. Chiquito found his land occupied by a Mexican family whom he convinced to vacate the premises by means of some forceful Apache persuasion. After an absence of seven years, Chiquito, now about seventy-five years old, began once again to create his Garden of Eden.[1]

Capitan Chiquito was present for the "Great Council at Old San Carlos" when William Garland, the railroad president, had a great feast for the whole reservation. The railroad had tried to convince the Apaches for years to allow the railroad to pass through the reservation on the way to Globe. The Great Council and feast was on February 8, 1898. There were fifteen cows roasted and coffee, flour, sugar, and tobacco was dispensed in large quantities. The San Carlos agent, Lieutenant Sedgewick Rice, was the facilitator of the meeting. The railroad president and his chief engineer, William Hood, represented the interests of the railroad. Chief Bylas was the main Apache spokesman, but Capitan Chiquito, Chief Cassadore, and others also had words to say. Although Capitan Chiquito had been away for many years, his story was known by the Apache and it was a respected, or at least infamous, legend among them.

Lieutenant Rice was especially instrumental in convincing the Apaches to compromise. This is most likely why the place where the railroad goes through San Carlos today was once known as Rice. The railroad paid the Apaches $8,000 for the land of the right-of-way and also agreed to allow the Apaches to ride the trains for free for thirty years. Yet they were not allowed to ride in the passenger cars, but only in the box cars of the freight trains.[2]

In 1898 Edward E. Ayer, the president of the Field Museum in Chicago, commissioned his nephew, Elbridge Ayer Burbank, to travel to Fort Sill in Oklahoma Territory to paint Geronimo. E. A. Burbank was born in Harvard, Illinois, and began his art training at the Academy of Design in Chicago, and then continued his art studies in Munich, Germany, from 1886 to 1892. After painting seven portraits of Geronimo, Burbank traveled to the San Carlos Apache Reservation and painted Chief Capitan Chiquito, Chief Talkalai, Chief Santo, and others. He eventually painted over 1,200 portraits of Apache, Navajo, Hopi, Cheyenne, Sioux, and other native tribes. In Capitan Chiquito's portrait he wears the red bandana that was worn by Apache scouts to distinguish them from the renegade Apaches that they fought against. Burbank wrote of his experience at San Carlos:

> One day while I was talking to an old Indian I mentioned the Apache Kid. He said that the Kid was still alive, though an old man, and that he knew where he lived. He had changed his name and called himself Is-niz-zi.[3]

As Chiquito began once again to dig the irrigation ditches for his orchards, he became involved in a water rights dispute with an African American man by the name of David Waldon, who lived downstream from him. Waldon began a letter-writing campaign to the San Carlos

Indian agent trying to convince him to return Chiquito to the reservation. Waldon pointed out over and over again in several letters how Chiquito had been on the warpath with the Apache Kid and was involved in the murder of Augustine Ruiz near his home. Waldon portrayed Chiquito as a nuisance who made liquor for other Indians in the canyon. In one of Waldon's letters, he writes:

> He [Chiquito] has been the cause of my having one law suit. He has induced two Indian families to squat above him. His presence in the canyon will ever be a menace to the peace and quiet of the neighborhood. The fact of his having joined the Kid on the warpath, from this identical spot. And having murdered one man almost within view of his present home will ever remain an obstacle to his regaining the faith and confidence of the people of this section of the country. An appeal to the Dept. at Washington for his removal would receive the support of 99 per cent of our citizens, but believing that the commanding officer at San Carlos, having the power, and knowing the facts of my controversy with Chiquito, would order his return to the reservation, have restrained from taking such a step—If he attempts to use water that is lawfully mine I will cause his arrest and prosecution.[4]

Chiquito defended himself and his time spent with the Apache Kid in a letter to the San Carlos Indian agent in March 1901:

> I love my land here at the Arivaipa Canon and wish to live well and happy. I had never done any things wrong since I came here to the Aravaipa County and I never killed no man yet or else not steal any horses or cows yet. I always try to do what is right all I can. Even I never got drunk yet. The color man had wrote a letter to you about name Captain Chiquita. I am Chiquita here. The black man wrote bad letters about me just because the color man wishes to have all my farm. The color man just big liar, that all. That a long time ago the bad Indians had killed one Mexican here at the Aravaipa, but that I never did that. I never killed no Mexican or any white man yet. The black man just tell big story that all. He don't know anything about that. I guess he just heard about it and wrote about it to you. Maybe the black man had a dream and maybe he thought today so he hurry and wrote about it to you. Oh no, that long, long time ago about 10 years ago, the Indians had killed Mexican man here at the Aravaipa. Those Indians had try to killed me that time too and they drived me off from my happy home and from my family. If I didn't go they killed me long ago. I went with them from mountains to mountains but I didn't killed any men and didn't killed any cattle at all. Then I came back to San Carlos by myself because I am not the one a

bad man. Never killed men or never steal horses and cattle yet. I always buy cattle when I need it. I had plenty horses so I don't have to steal any horses. That stealing business don't help anybody at all. I know what I am doing here and every white man in this Country they knew all about me. They could tell you the true story about one Indian man name Captain Chiquita.[5]

In another letter, Chiquito states that Waldon intentionally destroyed his ditches and that "he has been mad at me for I want to get my own land. Sometime he gets shovels and tries to hit me and carry pistol around my house."[6]

In this same letter Chiquito states:

I am living for a long time and I want to die right here and I want to my land which the collard fellow had took away from me. For my boys which are in school yet.[7]

Chiquito's son, Dajida (now Alonzo Speeche), graduated from Carlisle in 1901. I have not found evidence of any of his other sons being in boarding school at this time, but Capitan Chiquito says he had "boys" in boarding school. More than likely his son John Bullis was given this name in boarding school. It is recorded in the 1910 census that his son Elin Chiquito could speak and write good English, so apparently Elin had been sent away after surviving the ordeal at Mount Vernon federal prison.

In a letter written by Capitan Chiquito on May 8, 1901, Chiquito writes:

He [Waldon] had been bother me for three years now. But I couldn't report to the Agent because I could not write or couldn't understand English at all. But now I have children to help me. I loose my farm half of it and I want to have back again.[8]

In a letter written by Chiquito's son, John Bullis, in May 1900 to the US Land Office in Tucson, John writes:

Well one of the white Americans want to help us too, and he has been in the valley for about 21 years and he said that he wanted to be a witness for us, and I hope you notify him so. There are many white people here know my father and wanted to help him out because he has been here so long and (does not) get anything from the government for about over 20 years and makes his own living like you.[9]

The white American that John was referring to was Emil Kielberg.

Emil Kielberg had immigrated to America in 1872 from Copenhagen, Denmark, to seek opportunities for a better life. After working for four years in California for gold mining companies with little advance in income, Emil traveled to southern Arizona where he heard there were new strikes of gold, silver, and copper. He worked for four years in mines all over southeastern Arizona, saving his money for his dream of a fruit farm. While working at a mine in Mammoth, he was told of a canyon called Aravaipa that was nearby and suitable for farming. Emil's first trip down Aravaipa Creek in 1880 struck him with awe at the beauty of the place, and joy at the possibilities for farming. Emil had saved enough money to begin to homestead 160 acres on the creek and build a small shack. He continued to work in the mines as he created his fruit farm.

Kielberg would have had to pass through Chiquito's land every time he went to work in the mine at Mammoth. His land was about five miles upstream from Capitan Chiquito's rancheria, so he, no doubt, learned a few things from Chiquito about farming successfully in the canyon. By 1885 Emil was able to send for his childhood sweetheart in Copenhagen and marry her. At the time of Chiquito's land and water rights dispute, Kielberg was famous for his prize peaches, apples, berries, and vegetables that he sold to restaurants in Tucson and Florence. He no longer had to work in the mines and hired others to help him with his crops.[10]

Kielberg wrote three letters to the San Carlos Indian agent between 1898 and 1900 defending Capitan Chiquito's character and his right to his land. Kielberg also visited the Land Office and the General Surveyor's Office in Tucson with Chiquito to help him acquire the rights to his land. In his first letter to the San Carlos agent, Kielberg writes:

> Allow me to say that this Indian Chicito is a very industrious old Indian, I have been living neighbors with him for 18 years, and have always found him feasible and I know him to Farm the land he lives on for 18 years.[11]

Another neighbor, George Cook, wrote the following defense of Chiquito's character to San Carlos:

> I can do no less than say for him that I have known him for more than 20 years, and have always considered him to be a good old Indian, perfectly kind and inoffensive in character, and a better man generally than some persons in his neighborhood who claim citizenship. He informs me that certain parties have been writing complaints about him

to San Carlos in order to get him taken back to San Carlos. I have heard considerable about this, and I know that these parties, or at least some of them, are very much interested in the matter. They want Chiquita's land and water and I hope that you will take no action in the matter without investigating.[12]

In Kielberg's second letter to the San Carlos agent, he writes:

They are at present laying claims to Chicito's ditch on the Northside of Creek. They also claim ditch on Southside of Creek, both belonging to Chicito, it is a simple matter to prove that Chicito and Wife has made those ditches, and I think he should be protected in his rights, as I stated in a former letter to you old Chicito is feasible and a hard worker, but he don't hardly know how to look for protection.[13]

In this same letter Kielberg writes:

Capitan Chiquito has been living on his Ranch for 27 years. I personally have known him to live here 18 years barring the time he was sent off.[14]

In Kielberg's final letter to the San Carlos agent, he states:

Capitan Chiquito, my friend, wishes me to state to you what I know in regards to his land on the Aravaipa, and I will say that I know him to be the party who has made the ditches that he claims, one on the South side of the Aravaipa Creek, and the other on the north side of said Creek, and I also know that he built a Adobe House on the Land that the Waldons are claiming on North side of Creek, and I know this Indian to live on the Land that he claims for 19 years, I will also say that I have always found him to be a good neighbor.[15]

It seems unlikely that David Waldon could write, as his letters to the San Carlos agent are in two different scripts. These letter writers were, no doubt, his supporters in the canyon, one of whom was very literate and had beautiful penmanship. In Waldon's letter to the San Carlos agent, Captain Nicholson, in June 1899 writes:

Captain, in my answer to your communication of the 13th regarding the Chiquito controversy I am under the impression that I failed to answer your statement that Chiquito positively denies ever having disposed of any of his rights on Aravaipa Canyon. I do not understand that his ability or privilege to dispose of his rights are an issue, but to disabuse your mind as to this old sinner's veracity, I would suggest that you write to the County Recorder at Florence, Pinal County. You will find a bill of sale executed before notary public Powell, signed by Chiquito and his wife Marie (by their marks, thus X) conveying all rights then possessed by them to Emil Kielberg. Mr. Kielberg has this bill of sale with the County Recorder's certificate. Attached, you will please notice that this is the 2nd sale, in lieu of none, as claimed by Chiquito. The very fact of this latter sale is the cause of the present trouble—Mr. Kielberg armed with Chiquito's authority attempted to control my water rights, he was promptly arrested and fined. This however does not end the controversy, the bill of sale still exists and will come to the surface each time the water supply becomes short, thus causing me an endless trouble and expense.

Had Chiquito returned here and quietly attempted to reestablish the faith that he so outrageously broke, he could at least have lived in peace. His present attempt to establish a cocouy [*sic*; author's note: cocuy is a distilled liquor] on the Aravaipa is looked upon with suspicion and uneasiness. He is creating an endeavor from which liquor will be supplied the other Indians. Only a few days since a drunken Indian was seen coming from the direction of his place. I was informed that the drunken Indian's name was Sergeant Jim, but of this I am not positive. There can be but one end to Capitan Chiquito's remaining away from the Reservation and that is murder. He is under no restraint or supervision, and his complicity in the past fully justifies this prediction.[16]

In spite of the slanders and accusations against Chiquito by his adversaries in Aravaipa Canyon, he apparently had some friends in high places. In a letter of February 1900 from the Department of the Interior in Washington, DC, from William A. Jones, the commissioner of Indian Affairs, there is a somewhat baffling and mysterious passage written about Chiquito, who had once been a federal prisoner:

> The office is desirous of aiding this Indian in securing title to his land and preventing trespass thereon, if possible to do so, as he once rendered valuable service to the Government, which fact is personally known to the office.

I can only imagine that this refers to Capitan Chiquito's service as a US Army scout, and his possible reception of the congressional Medal of Honor. The commissioner then goes on to site several circulars issued by the General Land Office that protect the rights of Indians living on allotted lands. He then states:

Should you call the attention of the trespassers to the instructions contained in this circular, it is thought that they would surrender the lands they may have in their possession, and desist from further trespass upon the Indian's rights.[17]

The letter chain to the San Carlos agent about this land rights controversy ends in 1902. It seems that David Waldon was most likely paid off by the government for his claim to Chiquito's land. In a letter from the United States Indian inspector in Chicago, Illinois, he writes:

I have recommended that the land that Chiquito now lives on be allotted to him and if a suitable amount of agricultural land can be secured on the Old Military Reservation to allot the children there or to purchase the land belonging to the negro with whom Chiquito has been having the trouble, and divide it among Chiquito's children. To buy the negro out would straighten out the water trouble too, and get rid of that annoyance which would be quite an item.[18]

The US government, which had expelled Chiquito from his Aravaipa homeland on at least four occasions, had finally come to Capitan Chiquito's support; he had "once rendered valuable service to the Government."

15

Capitan Chiquito's Last Battle

AFTER THE RESOLUTION OF Capitan Chiquito's land and water rights dispute with David Waldon, Capitan Chiquito was left in relative peace for the remaining years of his life. His age was recorded as ninety-five in the US Census of 1910, which is perhaps a bit overestimated based on his recorded age of seventy in the Mount Vernon, Alabama, record of 1894 and the muster roll of Apache scouts, which said he was sixty in 1883.

Chiquito had fathered fifteen children, not including the ones killed in the Camp Grant Massacre, yet by 1910 only three sons were living. His son, Rex Chiquito, had died the year before the census. His remaining sons were John Bullis, Alonzo Speeche, and Elin Chiquito. Rex and Elin retained the last name of Chiquito, since they had remained with Chiquito at the Mount Vernon prison and had not been sent away to boarding school. Elin was two years old and Rex six when they went with their father to federal imprisonment. Capitan Chiquito had at least one child that did not survive the Mount Vernon ordeal.

Children in boarding school were given the names of army officers, writers, presidents, and sometimes characters from fiction. There are many families on the San Carlos Reservation today bearing the names of army officers: Howard, Grant, Dudley, Miles.

Chiquito's son, John, was ironically given the name of the very man who sent his father to prison: San Carlos agent Captain John Bullis.

Eventually, Chiquito's sons, Alonzo Speeche and Elin Chiquito, also took the name of Bullis. I told Velma that I thought it would be more appropriate for her to use her clan name and be known as Velma Tsejine, instead of Velma Bullis. In an 1896 document that bears the signatures of 640 San Carlos Apache men, 95 percent marked their names as an *X* and retained their Apache names. The ones that had gone to boarding schools and signed their names had names like Mark Twain, Charles Dickens, and Grover Cleveland.[1]

About 1910, John Bullis worked as a wagon driver hauling ore from the mines near the old mining town of Aravaipa. He apparently did not spend as long in boarding school as his brother, Alonzo, because his writing abilities were not as perfected.[2] Chiquito's son, Elin, farmed in Aravaipa and was also later the head carpenter at the San Carlos Agency. He was able to speak and write good English.[3]

When Alonzo Speeche graduated from the Carlisle Indian School in Pennsylvania in 1901, he had been away from his father and Apache land for eleven years and had never known life on the San Carlos Apache Reservation. He did not return to Apache land after his graduation but spent five years in Philadelphia. His memories of Apache land would be about Aravaipa Canyon.

According to Alonzo, he was kind of "wild" in these times and "lost in the valley of sin," no doubt wanting to learn something about life away from the strict confines of boarding school.[4] This boy, who once rode with his father and the Apache Kid, had been somewhat re-created by the boarding school system. He obtained employment as a machinist in a factory in Philadelphia, and he also played in the orchestra for movie theaters, as he had been part of the band at Carlisle.

About 1906 Capitan Chiquito's son Alonzo met a young lady named Vera Pickett, who was to become my wife's grandmother. Alonzo possibly met Vera while playing for the orchestra at the Walnut Street Theater in Philadelphia, where Vera and her sister had a burlesque act and were known as the Fontaine Sisters. Vera also later performed in Wild West shows as a kind of Annie Oakley character. It is said that she could pick up a handkerchief off the ground with her teeth while galloping by on her horse.[5] My wife's father, Lonnie, was born in Philadelphia in 1907 when Vera was seventeen. A year later Alonzo and Vera had another child named Audrey.

Lonnie told me that his father basically kidnapped him and Audrey from their mother when he was four years old, so Lonnie, like his father, was estranged from his mother at a young age. Lonnie's father, Alonzo, stayed with friends in Chicago for a while before he decided to return to Apache land with his children after an absence of about twenty years. Vera was not able to locate her children or establish a relationship with them again until they were in their early twenties. Alonzo reestablished his relationship with his father, Chiquito, and brothers and had an eighteen-acre farm at Old San Carlos. Lonnie says that he and Audrey "learned to talk the Apache language, lived their way and learned their culture."[6]

In March 1911, Alonzo assisted his father, Capitan Chiquito, with his application for an allotment of 160 acres of land, which included the massacre site. Alonzo testified that he had frequently walked over the land on which his father had settled and there was no gold, silver, copper, or other minerals suitable for mining. Alonzo's brother, Elin Chiquito, also made an allotment application for 160 acres of land next to his father's land and was granted a patent to it in 1916. Elin and Alonzo regularly visited their father from Old San Carlos on horseback. Alonzo eventually was also patented 160 acres of land in Aravaipa canyon.[7]

In 1915 Alonzo wrote the superintendent at the Carlisle Indian School, Mr. Lipps, requesting admission there for my father-in-law, Lonnie, and his sister, Audrey. His family still went by the last name of Speeche. The surname of Bullis was not taken by the family until shortly before Capitan Chiquito's death. Alonzo writes in an artistic penmanship:

> DEAR SIR, I seek admission to your school for my two motherless children, Lon Randolph Speeche, boy, age 8, and Audrae Speeche, girl, age 7. Both has attended kindergarten school of Phoenix and two years at Rice Indian School, Rice, Arizona [Authors note: Rice is now downtown San Carlos]. At present they are attending Rice school. Dr. Perkins is the superintendent. Since they are motherless and I have no mother also to care for them, they should be given training and education at Carlisle. Why Carlisle? Because I got my training and education there, class 1901. I have reason to desire to have them under her charge. It is through Carlisle's training that I am mining and civil engineer. My work requires considerable territory and my children are forever neglected in my

absence. Vincent Nat-alish, class 1900 of Carlisle is going to New York City about the 1st of October. He agrees to take my children to Carlisle if the admissions is O.K. Mr. Vincent Nat-alish is stationed at Rice Indian School. Please advise me of their transportation from Rice, Arizona, if your decision is favorable. Enclosed photo of children. We are Apaches.

Respectfully Yours, Alonzo Speeche.[8]

Alonzo received a reply from the superintendent of Carlisle dated September 7, 1915, which basically said that Carlisle no longer accepted children under the age of sixteen and he could reapply when they were of that age.[9]

In 1917 Alonzo married an Apache lady by the name of Jane Kidde, who, no doubt, assisted him in raising his children. With Jane he had two other children. One little girl died at the age of three, possibly from the flu. When Jane was asked the child's name at an inheritance hearing, she replied that the child had no name—a very odd thing to say of a child of three, but perhaps this had to do with the Apache custom of not speaking the names of the dead. The other child, Dorothy, lived into adulthood and had a son named Churchill. Lonnie's nephew, Churchill, was surely named after Winston during the war years; he later served in the US Army.[10]

Capitan Chiquito's last battle would not be with Mexicans, Americans, or African Americans, but with the deadliest pandemic in world history.

Historian John M. Barry writes:

In 1918 an influenza virus emerged—probably in the United States— that would spread around the world and would kill more people than any other outbreak of disease in human history. Epidemiologists today estimate that influenza likely caused at least fifty million deaths worldwide, and possibly as many as one hundred million. Symptoms were terrifying. Blood poured from noses, ears, eye sockets; some victims lay in agony; delirium took others away while living. Routinely two people in a single family would die. Three deaths in a family were not uncommon.[11]

Capitan Chiquito's neighbors, the Kielbergs, lost their twenty-five-year-old son, Emil Kielberg Jr., in November 1918; his fourteen-month-old son, Frederick, had died from the same flu four months earlier.[12] Capitan Chiquito's son, John, most likely died of influenza, as he was said to have died shortly before his father.[13] Capitan Chiquito and his two surviving sons, Alonzo and Elin, may have taken the surname Bullis at this time in honor of their brother, John Bullis. Alonzo begins to sign his name Alonzo S. Bullis about this time. There is no reference to Chiquito as Bullis, until after his death.

According to Jeanette Cassa, granddaughter of Apache Chief Juh, Capitan Chiquito spent his last days helping other Apaches who had contracted the virus.[14]

Ian Record remarks about his interviews with Apache elders: "Cassa and other elders lament that many Aravaipa and Pinal descendants look to Geronimo, a Chiricahua, rather than Hashke Bahnzin [Eskiminzin] or Capitan Chiquito, as their most prominent ancestor, which they believe reflects their ignorance about ancestral Aravaipa and Pinal places."[15]

There are many Apache grave sites on the north side of Aravaipa Creek on the Chiquito allotment that are said to be the burial places of influenza victims. Capitan Chiquito most likely employed the "gray medicine" (*izeelibahe*: desert lavender) in his healing rituals. In Apache medical use of herbs, the rituals and prayers that were used in healing were just as important, or more so, than the properties of the plant itself. According to botanist Seth Pilsk, the "gray medicine" saved many Apache people, whereas many non-Apache people in the canyon died from the disease.[16]

Capitan Chiquito's former wife, Josepha, stated that on May 17, 1919: "He [Chiquito] was caring for his fruit trees and took sick and died right away."[17] In the literature of the time it was reported that there were "a number of cases where people were perfectly healthy and died within twelve hours."[18]

Two or three months before Chiquito's death, he was visited by the inspector in charge of Indian affairs, John J. Terrill, who writes:

> Captain Chiquito departed this life about one month hence, at an extreme old age, supposed between 100 to 103 years old. He claims to have been between 10 and 12 years old when that most remarkable phenomena, the falling of the stars occurred, which as I recall was 1833. This old Indian is buried within a few yards from his Indian home, in which he recently died.[19]

Capitan Chiquito's only remaining wife, Mary, who had spent the years in prison with him, died about two months after him, probably of the flu, or of a broken heart. She was the young Mohave girl (at least forty years younger than him) that he had captured as a child, who had stood by him to the end.[20] A trust patent to Capitan Chiquito's land was finally issued to his heirs on March 26, 1920, ten months after his death.[21]

And so ended the remarkable and adventurous life of Capitan Chiquito: an Apache warrior, American army scout, gifted farmer, and healer. He bravely battled Mexican and American invaders of his homeland. He traveled to Washington, DC, with a delegation of Apache chiefs and met with President Grant. For a time he was a fugitive with the renegade Apache Kid, and then he suffered in a federal prison with the notorious Geronimo. Upon his release he reclaimed his land on Aravaipa Creek and successfully gained ownership of the site of the infamous Camp Grant Massacre in which two of his wives perished. Because he was a gifted agriculturalist, he at one time had six wives who assisted him with his vegetables and fruit orchard. He spent his last days heroically assisting Apache influenza victims at the cost of his own life.

One of Capitan Chiquito's great-granddaughters, Deana Reed, said this to me about her great-grandfather: "As I became more immersed in the history of Capitan Chiquito's time and familiar with his stories, a picture of him began to form. This was a man with a larger view which enabled him to move with the times amid a great shift of cultural changes. He was a shape-shifter."

Around the time of Chiquito's death, his son Dajida (Alonzo) was converted to Christianity by Lutheran missionaries at San Carlos. He was given the Gospel of John to read, which played a great part in his conversion. Alonzo gave to two of the missionaries a photo story of his conversion, in which he calls himself, "Dajida, the ancient arrow maker." This story was written in a 1930 edition of the Lutheran newsletter the *Apache Scout*. Alonzo writes:

> Dajida decides to look into the white man's books for better ways. From college he brings home a diploma, "big game." Spiritually he was still wild. Dajida learned the white man's worldly pleasures and is lost in the valley of sin.

Alonzo was adept at making arrows and bows, and apparently loved to hunt. He included photos of himself making arrows, and writes:

> Dajida prays to snakes, whirlwind, nayanazani to bless his hunt, but mostly returns empty handed, and is angry at the three gods on account of their weakness. Dajida, after forty years in the wilderness of sin, emerges. He searched the scriptures for the real knowledge and finds

the Messiah, the true light. Dajida finds through the Gospel, that the worship of snakes, whirlwind, "nayanazani," and the white man's pleasures of the world is the same as praying to a fence post.

Nayanazani is one of the most important of the Diyin, the Holy Beings. He is the son of Changing Woman (a female sacred being) and the Sun. His life and exploits are the basis for many Apache stories, songs, and ceremonies. He is the model for all proper behavior of an Apache man.

Alonzo would become an interpreter of the gospel for the Lutheran missionaries. In the final photo in his album he is shown with a Bible in his hand pointing to the heavens, and he writes: "Dajida, Lon S. Bullis, today rejoices in the Lord Jesus Christ. Joy brought to him by the Lutheran missionaries. He interprets to an Apache congregation."[22]

Alonzo sent both of his children off to be educated by the Lutherans. His pastor writes: "His ardent desire was that his children should become well educated witnesses to Christ." His pastor celebrated communion with Alonzo at his bedside shortly before his death. He said Alonzo was smiling and cheerful and holding his hand; Alonzo said: "Farewell, then, till we meet again at the Savior's throne, Who has called us into His Kingdom and soon will call me hence."[23]

Alonzo was buried at the Phoenix Sanitarium Cemetery, which is now under a parking lot near the present Phoenix Indian Medical Center. He left his 160 acres at Aravaipa Canyon to his children: Lonnie, Audrey, and Dorothy. Alonzo also gave a little framed building of his to the Lutheran Church; he used to sell soft drinks in that building. He said that he hoped it could be used by the church for a library, because, "It is my desire to help overcome the superstition of my people."[24] There were only two religious denominations on the reservation at this time: the Lutherans and the Catholics. There are many different Christian churches on the reservation at this present time, yet the Lutherans are the only ones that forbid their members to take part in traditional Apache ceremonies, such as the Sunrise Dance.

Lonnie was at Martin Luther College in New Ulm, Minnesota, studying to be a minister when he received the news of his father's death. Tuberculosis, probably acquired at Carlisle, finally caught up with Alonzo, and he died in a Tuberculosis Sanitarium in Phoenix, Arizona, on July 11, 1924, at the age of forty-two.

Lonnie writes about his seminary training that he "couldn't hack it so I just dropped out. They threw Greek, Hebrew and Latin language at me and I wasn't even a High School graduate!"[25] Yet Lonnie told me that the real reason for leaving the Lutheran seminary was that they did not tell him of his father's death, until a year after it occurred. I'm sure it was more of his father's wish for him to be a minister, and not a dream of his own.

After leaving the seminary, Lonnie went to Kenosha, Wisconsin, where he had once attended the Evangelical Lutheran Friedens Church School. Lonnie writes of his years from 1925 to 1927:

> Came back to Kenosha, Wisconsin and just worked at the following companies: First at Nash Motor Car Company and then Cooper Underware Company as they needed me to play baseball in the City League. Made good money too for just a kid. Also played basketball in the City League and did alright for this Apache Indian.[26]

At the age of twenty, Lonnie decided to go to the Haskell Institute, a school for Native Americans in Lawrence, Kansas, to complete his high school education. After graduation, he was chosen with a group of ten to go to Lansing, Michigan, for training as a mechanic in a program that Haskell sponsored.

Lonnie was a strikingly handsome young man with a great sense of humor, although somewhat ribald. He was popular with the ladies and well-liked by people in general. After two years of this training, Lonnie said that the Depression dried up the money for the program, so he returned to Haskell to be trained as a printer. When he completed this two-year program, he stayed on at Haskell for another year as a student assistant on a salary.

Lonnie's mother, Vera, had managed to locate her children sometime during their twenties. I believe their father may have told them that their mother was dead, as Lonnie writes in one narrative: "My father brought my sister and I back to Arizona when my mother died."[27] His sister, Audrey, was living with her mother in Philadelphia at this time, and Lonnie decided to join them for a while. Vera had married a man named Howard Bensinger, who worked for many years with the John B. Stetson Hat Company. Lonnie stayed in Philadelphia about one year before deciding to return to San Carlos after an absence of sixteen years. In San Carlos Lonnie was hired as a rod man on a surveying team with the

Tribal Conservation Department. He worked this job for a year before taking a job on the White Mountain Apache Reservation, north of San Carlos. He worked at the Theodore Roosevelt School as a boy's adviser and athletic coach.

While working on the White Mountain Reservation, Lonnie fell in love with a non-Apache schoolteacher named Hazel Foster. Hazel was from San Diego, California. After graduating from a college in Flagstaff, she took a job teaching at the Theodore Roosevelt School. Lonnie visited her home in San Diego, but Hazel's parents were against their marriage. However, Hazel bore him a son, whom she named Lonnie. Lonnie Bullis was not to see his son until he was in his late eighties.

Hazel later married a marine named Joe W. Hemphill, who had survived Iwo Jima and fought in the Korean War. Hazel never had any other children besides Lonnie Hemphill. Lonnie Hemphill told me that his mother once asked him, "If you could be any kind of Indian, what kind would you want to be?" Lonnie answered, "An Apache!" His mom answered somewhat emotionally, "That is who you are." Lonnie Hemphill did not know who his father was until after the death of his mother. He came out to the San Carlos Apache Reservation in the 1990s to establish his Apache tribal membership, and he was amazed to find his father still alive. His father helped Lonnie with his tribal enrollment.

Lonnie Bullis was a wanderer in these days, constantly pulling up stakes and moving on. Perhaps embittered by his tragic love affair, he left the Theodore Roosevelt School after two years. In 1938 he went to Clinton, Oklahoma, and attended the Keen Business College. About this time he met another lady, named Pearl Butschli, who he married. They had a boy named DeWayne, born in Thomas, Oklahoma, but their marriage did not last long. When Lonnie finished the Keen Business College he was hired by the Swift Poultry Company as an accountant. Lonnie was employed by this company for thirty-two years. When the Swift Company transferred Lonnie to Yoakum, Texas, he left his wife and little boy behind.

Lonnie's son, DeWayne, said that he never forgave his father for leaving them. DeWayne was raised in the country by his grandparents, because Indians were looked down on in the city. DeWayne said his grandfather (E. T. Butschli) was the meanest man he ever knew; E. T. was ashamed of him because he was Indian, he said, yet his grandmother always stood up for him. Lonnie told me that his wife's old German father,

E. T., once tried to hit him in the head with a bucket. He obviously was not happy with his daughter's marriage to an Apache. When it was time for DeWayne to go to school, he told everyone that he was Mexican. Yet DeWayne had the heart to visit his father in his older years and attend his funeral. Abandonment issues are passed down through the generations. Lonnie Bullis was separated from his mother at a tender age, as was his father.

In Yoakum, Texas, Lonnie made friends with the Garrett family. The Garretts had three boys and three girls. He liked to drink with the boys, but, I believe, he was more interested in their three sisters. When the Swift Company transferred Lonnie to Grinnell, Iowa, one of the Garrett girls followed him. At the age of forty, Lonnie married Eva Garrett in 1947. Lonnie and Eva had two girls: Deana and my wife, Velma. This was to be one of the most stable times in Lonnie's life. He raised his girls in Clinton, Iowa, and lived in Iowa for twenty-five years.

Deana and Velma knew nothing about their colorful Apache heritage. Their dad never talked about it. Deana and Velma lived in an all-white neighborhood and graduated from Clinton High School. They were both cheerleaders at their school and quite popular. Their friends from high school today describe them as being beautiful and exotic, but they say they had no idea of their Apache background. When their dad retired from the Swift Company on his birthday (July 29) at the age of sixty-six, he found it hard to live with his wife, Eva. Once again, Lonnie would re-create his life and move back to San Carlos.[28]

Epilogue

My Life after the Reservation (Seven Years After)

I BEGAN MY STORY with Lonnie Bullis returning to the Apache Reservation for the final period of his life, and I will end it there. The decisions a person makes change many other people's lives and not just their own, and Lonnie's return to San Carlos surely changed mine. Although I am not a professional historian, I have tried my best to tell the story well and to tell it accurately. In my Indians of North America class at Texas A&M University, which I took as part of my undergraduate degree in anthropology, my professor felt he knew something about the Zuni Indians after doing field work there for six months. Well, after spending twenty-one years living and working with the Apaches, I still feel like I am an outsider looking in.

After Velma's death I stayed alone in our home at San Carlos for one year to write this story and to put closure on my life there. I was once told that our home was built on the site of an old Apache graveyard, yet we were never bothered by spirits and they seemed at peace with us being there.

Velma used to cry about everything, and I would always tell her that she should not watch the news as it often left her in tears. I was always much more stoic and did not show my emotions very much, but after being with Velma when she died I think I cried for about two years.

Velma's passage really changed me spiritually somehow, and I often feel her presence. She has left me a much more tender person, I think, and I often find tears rolling down my cheeks during sad movies or sad news, the same as what happened to her. I see this as evidence that her essence is with me.

One thing I have learned from my departed wife and her adventurous kinfolk is not to be afraid to start my life over again and to re-create myself. When I left San Carlos six years ago, I moved to our family ranch near Navasota, Texas. My parents were both in their nineties and needed help with their health and maintaining the ranch. My Dad died in our ranch house in 2015. Mom also died recently, at age ninety-six while in our home on hospice.

My fascination with Native Americans is probably only matched by my fascination with the Chinese. After all, the first Americans came here from northeast Asia over 12,000 years ago. I began taking Tai Chi, Mandarin Chinese, and Chinese calligraphy at the Confucius Institute at Texas A&M University. It was through friends at the Confucius Institute that I met a lady who was a widow and physician like myself.

She had just graduated from a medical university in China when she became pregnant with her second child. Because of China's "One Child" policy, she was told by Communist Party officials to abort her child or face consequences. She and her husband decided to keep the child, and she hid in a cousin's house until the childbirth. She thought she would only be punished with a fine, but she also lost her job at the hospital. One day a van arrived at her home and she was forcibly taken away after they knocked her husband to the ground. She was taken to a local hospital and given a mandatory tubal ligation.

I am not mentioning her name or the university of her graduation to protect her and her family from the Chinese Communist Party.

Her husband was under much pressure as the only wage earner in the family, yet he found some solace in attending an underground Christian church. Unfortunately, during one of the Christian services, the police came and beat him and took him to jail for attending an unauthorized Christian church. After his release from jail, he had to report to the police station every day for "rehabilitation." The police kept demanding more and more money from him, and he finally had to flee to America to seek political asylum. In California, after much hard work and worry about his family, his immune system failed and he died of leukemia. His wife came to America two weeks before his death. She was with him every day and said all she could do was faint and cry when he took his last breath. She was also seeking political asylum when I met her. Her son and daughter had stayed in China in the care of her husband's parents.

We were married in December 2016. We had only known each other for six months, but I guess it seemed right.

When her children were finally granted permanent residence status by the United States, I went to Beijing, China, to bring them to America. Their mother was not able to go, because she did not have her green card at that time and would not be allowed back in the United States.

I had been to Beijing before so I was not anxious about bringing back her twelve-year-old son and nine-year-old daughter. I first met them and their grandparents in a subway station in Beijing. The grandparents were very sad to see them go, because they were still mourning the death of their only son. When I walk the streets of Beijing, I see many people that would look right at home on the San Carlos Apache Reservation.

My mother always called my new wife "La La." I have no idea where she came up with that name, but in Mandarin it means "spicy hot." La La was my mother's primary caretaker over the last two years of her life, and her medical knowledge was a great help to her. Now that my mother has passed away, we are planning on moving to Tucson, Arizona, after we sell our family ranch. We will start a medical clinic there.

I took La La to San Carlos one time for the First Communion of my Apache goddaughter's daughter, Lorena. I have visited my god daughter, Melissa, also for the Sunrise Dance for her daughter at her "coming of age" ceremony. I am happy that people are living in my old home who are part of my family and who take care of the many trees that I planted. La La seemed to like Arizona, but she kept asking me, "Where are all the people?" I am looking forward to living in Arizona again and being near my Apache and non-Apache friends there. We will often visit the monastery where Velma is buried. I have bought a grave site next to Velma.

When my body is dead and in the ground, my skull and bones will lie next to Velma's until they are dust.

APPENDIX 1

Genealogy of Capitan Chiquito's Descendants

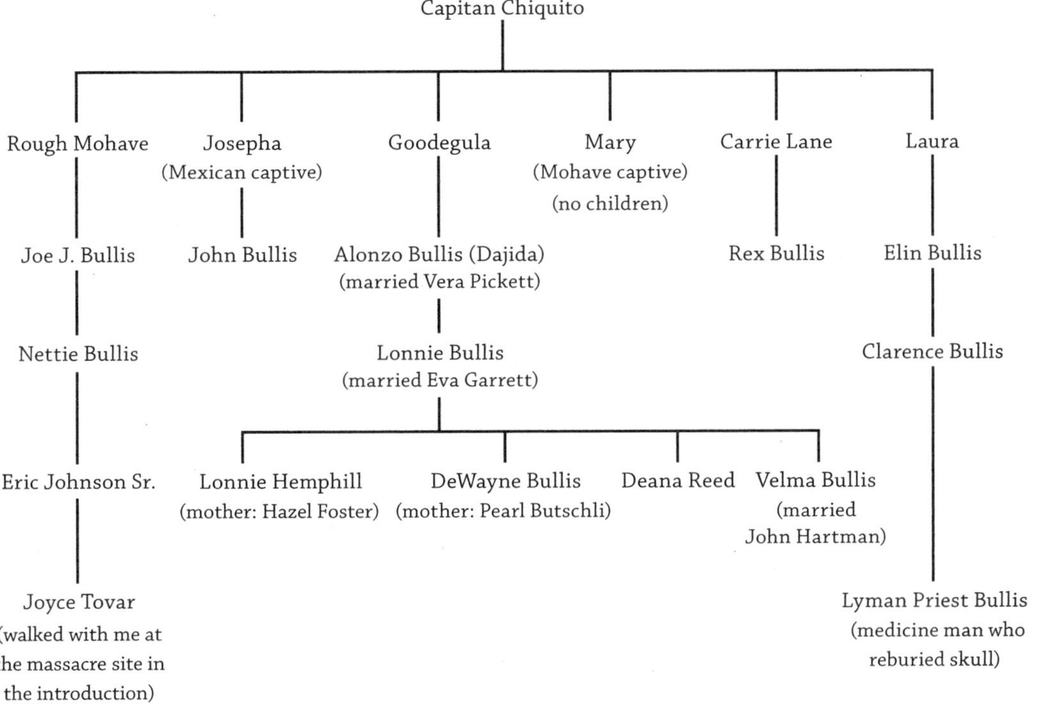

APPENDIX 2

Timeline of Events in the Life of Capitan Chiquito

1750 Aravaipa Canyon becomes an Apache stronghold when the Apache force the Sobaipuri Indians away.

1821 Capitan Chiquito born in Aravaipa Canyon.

Mexico wins Independence from Spain.

1830 Mexican captain Antonio Comaduran and his soldiers kill two Apache hunters near the mouth of Aravaipa Canyon.

1832 Mexican soldiers attack Apaches at Aravaipa canyon killing seventy-one Apache warriors and taking thirteen captives. They also took 216 horses and mules.

1840s The Mexican provinces of Sonora and Chihuahua offer a bounty for Apache scalps of men, women, and children.

1847 Antonio Comaduran and soldiers attack Aravaipa Canyon, killing sixteen warriors, seven women, and four boys. They took fourteen prisoners.

1848 After the Mexican-American War the Treaty of Guadalupe Hidalgo gives the United States New Mexico and the Arizona land below the Gila River.

1854   With the Gadsden Purchase, the United States gave Mexico $10 million dollars to acquire parts of Arizona that included the city of Tucson and the Apache lands.

1861   Ramon Elias is killed by Apaches he is pursuing to retrieve stolen cattle.

1863   Aravaipa, Pinal, and Chiricahua Apache attack San Xavier del Bac mission in Tucson and take over 100 cattle belonging to Juan Elias. Juan's brother Cornelio is killed pursuing the Apaches.

Jesus Maria Elias leads an attack on Aravaipa Canyon to avenge the death of his brothers, and fifty Apache people are killed.

1867   An Apache assassin shoots Juan Elias with a shotgun full of mescal seeds as he sleeps outside his home. As he is recovering from wounds to his back and neck, the ranch is again attacked and two workmen are killed.

1869   Colonel Reuben Bernard, Colonel John Green, and other army officers begin search-and-destroy missions to kill Apaches and destroy their food supplies.

Aravaipa Apaches attack a wagon train at Oracle.

1871   Jesus Maria Elias leads another attack on the Aravaipa Apaches in what came to be known as the Camp Grant Massacre.

The Apache make several revenge attacks; Vincent Colyer is sent by President Grant to try to make a peace agreement.

Dr. Valery Havard takes an Apache woman's skull from the massacre site and sends it back east.

1872   In a new effort to make peace with the Apache and establish a reservation, President Grant sends General Otis Howard to Apache land.

General George Crook begins his campaign to subdue the Indians who refused to stay on reservations. In the battle of Skull Cave he uses Apache scouts to attack the Yavapai Indians.

1873   San Carlos Apache Reservation established.

Capitan Chiquito enlists as an army scout, possibly to assist General Crook in arresting those who killed the officer in command at San Carlos, Lieutenant Jacob Almy.

1874   Capitan Chiquito deserts the army January 31 after Yavapai Indians at San Carlos murder two freighters who refuse to give them more whiskey. He returns to San Carlos in August.

John Clum becomes the Indian agent at San Carlos.

1875   John Clum holds a trial for two Indians who attempted to assassinate Capitan Chiquito.

1876   John Clum and Apache scouts convince the Chiricahua Apaches to come to San Carlos.

John Clum takes a delegation of Apache chiefs to Washington, DC.

1877   John Clum and Apache scouts capture Geronimo and other Apache chiefs and bring them to San Carlos. Geronimo is freed after Clum resigns as San Carlos agent.

John Clum becomes the mayor of Tombstone and the editor of the *Tombstone Epitaph*.

Capitan Chiquito and Ezkiminzin return to Aravaipa.

1881   A medicine man at Cibecue begins a Ghost Dance to make the white people go away. In the attempt to arrest him, the medicine man and several soldiers are killed. This causes an uprising of Apaches and an attack on Fort Apache. Capitan Chiquito and wives return temporarily to Old San Carlos until the uprising is over.

1883   Capitan Chiquito enlists as a scout in Company F of the US Army.

1884   Capitan Chiquito transfers to Company B under Lieutenant Britton Davis.

1885   From May to August Capitan Chiquito is in Mexico pursuing Geronimo under Lieutenant Britton Davis.

He resigns from the army in August when they return to San Carlos.

1886   Geronimo surrenders to General Miles and is sent with other Chiricahua to Fort Marion, Florida.

1887   The army scout Apache Kid becomes a renegade after avenging the death of his grandfather. He is sent to the federal prison at Alcatraz.

1888   Ezkiminzin's ranch is raided by settlers who wanted his land. The Apache Kid is released from federal prison.

1889   The Apache Kid is arrested again and tried in Globe on state charges.

The Apache Kid and other prisoners kill Sheriff Glenn Reynolds and his deputy on the way to Yuma Territorial Prison.

1890   Capitan Chiquito leaves Aravaipa with the Apache Kid, and Indian agent Captain John Bullis has friends and relatives of the Apache Kid arrested.

Capitan Chiquito turns himself in and is imprisoned in the Old San Carlos guardhouse.

1891   Capitan Chiquito and other Aravaipa families are imprisoned at Fort Union, New Mexico.

1892   Capitan Chiquito, Eskiminzin, and forty-four other Aravaipa Apaches are sent to Mount Vernon Barracks, Alabama, to be imprisoned with Geronimo and the Chiricahua Apaches.

Capitan Chiquito's son, Dajida, is sent to the Grand Junction Indian School in Colorado and is given the name Alonzo Speeche.

1894   The Chiricahua Apaches are sent to Fort Sill, Oklahoma, in October; later that year Capitan Chiquito and the Aravaipa Apaches are allowed to return to San Carlos.

1897   Capitan Chiquito and other families are allowed to return to Aravaipa. While Capitan Chiquito was gone, David Waldon claimed portions of his land, and they begin a land dispute.

1898   Capitan Chiquito is present for the Great Council at Old San Carlos when the Apaches make a deal with the railroad president to allow the train to pass through the reservation.

Capitan Chiquito has his portrait painted by Elbridge Ayer Burbank.

1900   David Waldon and friends write letters to the San Carlos Indian agent trying to have Capitan Chiquito evicted from Aravaipa because of his association with the Apache Kid.

Capitan Chiquito and his supporters also write letters to defend his character.

The commissioner of Indian Affairs decides in favor of Capitan Chiquito, writing that Chiquito "once rendered valuable service to the government."

1901   Capitan Chiquito's son, Alonzo Speeche (Dajida), graduates from Carlisle Indian school and is employed as a machinist in a factory in Philadelphia.

1906   Alonzo Speeche meets Vera Picket while playing for the orchestra at the Walnut Street Theater.

Vera and her sister had a burlesque act there and were known as the Fontaine Sisters.

1907   Lonnie Randolph Speeche is born in Philadelphia to Alonzo
Speeche and Vera Picket. Lonnie's last name is eventually
changed to Bullis.

1908   Alonzo and Vera have another child and name her Audrey.

1910   Alonzo takes his children and goes to Old San Carlos; Vera did
not find her children again until they were adults.

1911   Alonzo assists his father, Capitan Chiquito, with his application
for an allotment of 160 acres of land that included the massacre
site.

1918   The influenza pandemic begins to take lives in Aravaipa Canyon. Capitan Chiquito helps other Apaches who are sick with
the influenza.

1919   On May 17, while caring for his fruit trees, Capitan Chiquito
suddenly becomes sick with influenza and dies the same day.

NOTES

CHAPTER 1

1. Kielberg-McClenahan 2013, 185.
2. Record 2008, 102–3.
3. Record 2008, 102.
4. Smith 1997, 103.
5. Basso 1979, 53.

CHAPTER 2

1. Olson 2009, 69.
2. Terrell 1919.
3. Morris 2002, 125.
4. Morris 2002, 191.
5. Clark 2001, 3.
6. Morris 2002, 155.
7. Seth Pilsk interview April 2014. Information from Hopi visiting Fort Apache.
8. Terrell 1972, 81.
9. Bolton 1936, 245.
10. Morris 2002, 299.
11. Santiago 2011, 58.
12. Santiago 2011, 92 and 193.
13. Netvig 1794, 82.
14. Terrell 1919.
15. Dobyns 1981, 21.
16. Bolton 1936, 363.
17. Bolton 1936, 519–20.
18. Worcester 1979, 14.
19. Moorhead 1968, 183–95; Griffen 1998, 60 and 62.
20. Velasco 1865, 85; Lockwood 1987, 31.

CHAPTER 3

1. Dobyns 1981, 16–26.
2. Griffen 1998, 6 and 55.
3. Record 2008, 53.
4. Griffen 1998, 13.
5. McCarthy 1997, 35–36.
6. Kessell 1976, 285.
7. Goodwin 1971, 257–97.
8. McCarty 1997, 41–52.
9. Officer 1987, 141–42.
10. Worcester 1979, 37–48.
11. Officer 1987, 206–7.
12. Jackson 1977, 23.
13. Goodwin 1971, 253–59; Terrell 1972, 274.

CHAPTER 4

1. Ogle 1970, 29.
2. Ogle 1970, xxi–xxii. In the introduction by Oakah L. Jones Jr.
3. Worcester 1979, 14 and 33.
4. Cozzens 2001, 156.
5. Cozzens 2001, 156; Wesley Merrit in *Harper's New Monthly Magazine* 80, no. 459 (April 1890): 725.
6. Ogle 1970, 34.
7. Kitch 1927.
8. Jacoby 2008, 82; email of Ramon Elias to John Hartman, December 30, 2014.
9. Jacoby 2008, 84; email of Ramon Elias to John Hartman, January 2, 2015.
10. Court of Claims Indian Depredations 1888, Testimony of Jesus Elias.
11. Email of Ramon Elias to John Hartman, December 30, 2014.
12. Court of Claims 1888. Juan Elias testimony, Indian Depredations.
13. Officer 1987, 306.

CHAPTER 5

1. Court of Claims 1888. Juan Elias testimony, Indian Depredations; "Reminiscences of Alvina Rosenda Contreras," 1927, Arizona Historical Society.
2. Terrell 1972, 261.
3. Danielson 1971, 61; Scott 1928, 183.
4. Terrell 1972, 247.
5. Russell 2003, 63–65.
6. Terrell 1972, 264.
7. Sweeney 1992, 1–2, 37–38.
8. Russell 2003, 66–68.

9. Bourke 1971, 53–54.
10. Van Orden and Barnes 2013, 319.
11. Cozzens 2001, 44.
12. Ogle 1970, 74–76.
13. Bourke 1971, 29.
14. Randall 1995, 58–60.

CHAPTER 6

1. Record 2008, 184.
2. Colyer 1871, 31. Letter of Lieutenant Royal Whitman to Colonel J. G. C. Lee, May 17, 1871.
3. Terrell 1972, 273–74.
4. Colyer 1871, 31. Letter of Lieutenant Royal Whitman to Colonel J. G. C. Lee, May 17, 1871.
5. *Weekly Arizonian*, March 11, 1871, 2.
6. Thrapp 1967, 83.
7. Record 2008, 193.
8. Colyer 1871, 34. Testimony of Dr. Conant B. Briesly to Captain William Nelson.
9. Notes of April 29, 1871, from Lieutenant Whitman's journal.
10. Worcester 1979, 121.
11. Schellie 1968, 24.
12. Schellie 1968, 123–25.
13. Record 2008, 230–31.
14. Reminiscences of Alvina Rosenda Contreras, 1927, 2.
15. Schellie 1968, 142–51.
16. Reminiscences of Sherman Curley, Arizona State Museum.
17. Haley 1997, 259–61; Colyer 1871, 32–34.
18. Reminiscences of Alvina Rosenda Contreras, 1927, 1–2.
19. Court of Claims, Indian Depredations, No. 7,550.

CHAPTER 7

1. Ball 1988, 26–27.
2. Randall 1995, 66–67.
3. Record 2008, 264.
4. Whitman 1871, journal entry of May 27, 1871.
5. Record 2008, 264.
6. Schellie 1968, 189.
7. Schellie 1968, 189–93; Worcester 1979, 125; *Prescott Courier*, April 18, 1921.
8. Worcester 1979, 123.
9. Thrapp 1967, 97.
10. Worcester 1979, 125–26; Schellie 1968, 175.

11. Museum of Fine Arts, Houston, Texas. *Scene of the Camp Grant Massacre* by Vincent Colyer. Accession Number B.2003.8.

12. Haley 1997, 270.

13. Whitman 1871, journal entry for September 10, 1871.

14. Colyer 1871, 14 and 36.

15. Colyer 1871, 15–17.

16. Colyer 1871, 17.

17. Colyer 1871, 17; Lieutenant Whitman's journal entry for September 19, 1871.

18. Jacoby 2008, 248.

19. Colwell-Chanthaphonh 2007, 71–73.

20. Online source: en.wikipedia.org/wiki/Valery_Havard.

21. Penfield 2004, 147–48.

22. Clum 1936, 81.

23. Whitman 1871, journal entry of September 10, 1871.

24. Terrell 1972, 293.

25. Terrell 1972, 294.

26. Howard 1907, 152.

27. Basso 1979, 57–58.

28. Howard 1872.

29. Cozzens 2001, 116; Howard 1907, 148–49.

30. Howard 1907, 148–49.

31. Record 2008, 273–74.

32. Record 2008, 275.

33. Jacoby 2008; www.brown.edu/Aravaipa, *The Treaty*: *Peace Negotiations Part 2*.

34. Howard 1907, 183–84; Jacoby 2008, 251.

35. Howard 1908, 79.

36. Jacoby 2008, 254.

CHAPTER 8

1. Thrapp 1967, 118.

2. Bourke 1971, 182.

3. Robinson 1949, 129.

4. Bourke 1971, 184.

5. Bourke 1971, 188–90.

6. Cozzens 2001, 149–50; and Worcester 1979, 152–54.

7. Burns 2010, 26; Dobyns 1981, 24.

CHAPTER 9

1. Terrell 1972, 306–7.

2. Ball 1980, 37.

3. Perry 1993, 119–20.

4. Register of Enlistments, Indian Scouts, Volume 150 (1866–1874).

5. Cozzens 2001, 234.

6. Haley 1997, 298–99; Worcester 1979, 162; Register of Enlistments, Indian Scouts, Volume 150 (1866–1874).

7. Radbourne 2005, 36–37.

8. *Nevada State Journal*, August 19, 1874.

9. Carmony 1997, 2–4.

10. Haley 1997, 301.

11. John Clum's Diary, Paper Drawer 1, Special Collections, University of Arizona Library.

12. Clum, Annual Report of the Commissioner of Indian Affairs for the year of 1875, 218; Burns 2010, 42.

13. Clum 1936, 172–74.

14. Clum 1936, 177–79.

15. Clum 1936, 185–87. This source applies to the following paragraphs as well.

16. Clum 1936, 188–95; Carmony 1997, 148–54.

CHAPTER 10

1. Clum 1936, 201–5.

2. Clum 1936, 206–22.

3 .Clum 1936, 226–54.

4. Clum 1936, 263.

5. Clum 1936, 254–58.

6. Clum 1936, 259.

CHAPTER 11

1. Goodwin 1969, 352–53 and 600–618.

2. Record 2008, 64.

3. Goodwin 1969, 351–52.

4. Jacoby 2008, 257–59.

5. Letter of James B. Kitch, July 28, 1927, Testimony in Case of Chiquito Bullis by Josepha Bullis.

6. Reminiscences of Alvina Rosenda Contreras, January 10, 1927, Arizona Historical Society.

7. Collins 1999, 32–69.

8. Worcester 1979, 247.

9. Collins 1999, 109.

10. Collins 1999, 160–61.

11. Collins 1999, 223–24.

12. Register of Enlistments . . . Indian Scouts, Vol. 153 (1882–86), C680.

13. Cozzens 2001, 406.

14. Cozzens 2001, 409.

15. Register of Enlistments, Indian Scouts, Vol. 153 (1882–86), C699.

16. Davis 1929, 149–93.

17. Register of Enlistments . . . Indian Scouts, Vol. 153 (1882–86), C680, C699, C722, C751, C772.

18. Record 2008, 306n21.

19. Letter of James B. Kitch, July 28, 1927, Testimony in Case of Chiquito Bullis by Sherman Curley.

20. Letter of James B. Kitch, July 28, 1927, Testimony in Case of Chiquito Bullis by Sherman Curley.

CHAPTER 12

1. McKanna 2009, 8, 9, and 13.

2. *The 1887 Sonora Earthquake*, Phil Pearthree; and Kielberg-McClenahan 2013, 57–58.

3. Burns 2010, 256–57.

4. De La Garza 1995, 28–29.

5. McKanna 2009, 55.

6. McKanna 2009, 61–62.

7. De La Garza 1995, 54–55.

8. Record 2008, 67–68.

9. De La Garza 1995, 63–64.

10. Hayes 1947, 47–49; De La Garza 1995, 87–96.

11. De La Garza 1995, 131; Letter of James B. Kitch July 28, 1927, Case of Chiquito Bullis by Josepha Bullis.

12. Letter of James B. Kitch July 28, 1927, Case of Chiquito Bullis by Josepha Bullis.

13. Forrest and Hill 1947, 120 and 121.

14. Meed 1993, 22.

15. Forrest and Hill 1947, 59.

16. *Arizona Daily Citizen*, September 15, 1890.

CHAPTER13

1. De La Garza: 1995, 109–15, 139.

2. Meed 1993, 26.

3. Interview with Seth Pilsk, coordinator of the San Carlos Elder's Council, 2013; Jacoby 2008, 262.

4. San Carlos Agency Records, Arizona Historical Society, M.S. 707 (box 7 of 18), Letterbooks 39 and 210.

5. Stockel 2004, 93–96.

6. Stockel 1993, 141.

7. Stockel 1993, 240.

8. Stockel 1993, 153.

9. Stockel 2004, 69.

10. Carlisle Indian School Descriptive and Historical Record of Student, National Archives Trust Fund; Letter of James B. Kitch July 28, 1927, Case of Chiquito Bullis by Josepha Bullis.

11. *Arizona Silver Belt*, Globe, Arizona, October 27, 1894.

12. Adams 1995, 215.

13. Adams 1995, 228.

14. Adams 1995, 237.

15. Stockel 1993, 178.

16. *Arizona Silver Belt*, September 1, 1894.

17. Stockel 1993, 183; Curly is Chiquito's nephew Sherman Curley.

18. Scott 1928, 183.

19. Record 2008, 106.

20. Interview with Mary O'Donnell, daughter-in-law of Alberta Kindelay, June 2014.

21. Scott 1928, 190.

CHAPTER 14

1. Letter of David Waldon to San Carlos agent Captain Nicholson, May 19, 1899, San Carlos Agency Records 1890–1930, box 6, folder 134, Arizona Historical Society.

2. Proceedings of the council held at San Carlos, Arizona, February 8, 1898, Negotiating with Indians for Right-of-Way; David Myrick, *Railroads of Arizona*, vol. 111, 1980.

3. Burbank 1944, 8–36.

4. Letters of David Waldon to the commanding officer of the San Carlos Indian Agency, September 30, 1898. San Carlos Agency Records, 1890–1930, box 6, folder 134, Arizona Historical Society.

5. Letter of Capitan Chiquito to the Indian agent at San Carlos, A.T., May 1901.

6. Letter of Capitan Chiquito to the Indian agent at San Carlos, A.T., March 16, 1900.

7. Letter of Capitan Chiquito to the Indian agent at San Carlos, A.T., March 16, 1900.

8. Letter of Capitan Chiquito to the Indian agent at San Carlos, A.T., May 8, 1901.

9. Letter of John Bullis to John H. Bauman, US Land Office, Tucson, Arizona, May 27, 1900.

10. Kielberg-McClenahan 2013, 3–52.

11. Letter of Emil Kielberg to the San Carlos agent, January 6, 1898, San Carlos Agency Records, 1890–1930, box 6, folder 134, Arizona Historical Society.

12. Letter of George Cook to the San Carlos agent, November 18, 1898, San Carlos Agency Records, 1890–1930, box 6, folder 134, Arizona Historical Society.

13. Letter of Emil Kielberg to the San Carlos agent, March 17, 1898, San Carlos Agency Records, box 6, folder 134, Arizona Historical Society.

14. Letter of Emil Kielberg to the San Carlos agent, March 17, 1898, San Carlos Agency Records, box 6, folder 134, Arizona Historical Society.

15. Letter of Emil Kielberg to the San Carlos agent, March 12, 1900, San Carlos Agency Records, box 6, folder 134, Arizona Historical Society.

16. Letter of David Waldon to Acting Indian Agent Captain W. J. Nicholson, June 11, 1899.

17. Letter from William A. Jones, Commissioner Office of Indian Affairs, to Capt. W. J. Nicholson, San Carlos Indian agent, February 28, 1900, San Carlos Agency Records, box 6, folder 134, Arizona Historical Society.

18. Letter from the US Indian inspector, Chicago, Illinois, to the San Carlos Indian agent, February 15, 1902, San Carlos Agency Records, box 6, folder 134, Arizona Historical Society.

CHAPTER 15

1. Letter from the Acting Secretary of the Interior, Washington, DC, March 24, 1896. *An agreement with the San Carlos Reservation Indians ceding certain lands to the United States, together with reports from the Commissioners of Indian Affairs and of the General Land Office, and a draft of a bill ratifying and confirming the agreement.*

2. Information from the US Census of 1910 and a letter written by John Bullis to the US Land Office in Tucson, AZ, on May 27, 1900.

3. US Census of 1910 and a letter from John J. Terrell, inspector in charge, San Carlos Agency to the Commissioner of the General Land Office, Washington, DC, June 24, 1919.

4. *The Apache Scout*, a newsletter of the San Carlos Lutheran Church, Vol. 8, April 1930, No. 2.

5. Information obtained from Vera's granddaughters Delores Russel and Judy Nolan in 2003.

6. Letter from Lonnie Bullis to his daughter, Deana (Bullis) Reed, 1985.

7. Indian Allotment Affidavit, US Land Office, Phoenix, AZ, March 6, 1911.

8. Letter of Alonzo Speeche to the superintendent of Carlisle Indian School, September 2, 1915.

9. Letter of Alonzo Speeche to the superintendent of Carlisle Indian School, September 2, 1915. Response.

10. Testimony of Jane Bullis in the case of Chiquito Bullis. Letter from Janes B. Kitch, July 28, 1927. Interview with Charlotte Suttle, daughter of Churchill Suttle, by the author in 2003.

11. Barry 2009, 4 and 224.

12. Kielberg-McClenahan 2013, 154–55.

13. Testimony of Josepha Bullis in the case of Chiquito Bullis, Letter of James Kitch, Indian Field Service, July 28, 1927.

14. Record 2008, 315n53.

15. Record 2008, 355n22.

16. Information from Seth Pilsk, coauthor of *Western Apache Trees and Shrubs*, on an herb walk in Aravaipa Canyon, April 2012.

17. Testimony of Josepha Bullis in the case of Chiquito Bullis, Letter of James B. Kitch, Indian Field Service, July 28, 1927.

18. Barry 2009, 242.

19. Letter of John J. Terrell, inspector in charge, to the San Carlos Agency, June 24, 1919.

20. Testimony of Josepha Bullis in the case of Capitan Chiquito, letter of James B. Kitch, Indian field agent, July 28, 1927.

21. Letter of E. B. Meritt, assistant commissioner to the office of Indian Affairs, Washington, DC, July 18, 1927.

22. *The Apache Scout*, a newsletter of the San Carlos Lutheran Church, Vol. 8, April 1930, No. 2.

23. *The Apache Scout*, a newsletter of the San Carlos Lutheran Church, Vol. 8, April 1930, No. 2.

24. Letter of Alonzo Bullis to the San Carlos Indian agent dated March 13, 1924.

25. Letter from Lonnie Bullis to his daughter, Deana (Bullis) Reed, 1985. Lonnie outlined his life story in a letter to Deana for her daughter, Stacy, for a college sociology class.

26. Letter from Lonnie Bullis to his daughter, Deana (Bullis) Reed, 1985.

27. Letter from Lonnie Bullis to his daughter, Deana (Bullis) Reed, 1985.

28. Letter from Lonnie Bullis to his daughter, Deana (Bullis) Reed, 1985; information from the DeWayne Bullis family, the Lonnie Hemphill family, Deana (Bullis) Reed, and Martha Logan, friend of Deana and Velma in high school.

BIBLIOGRAPHY

ARCHIVAL SOURCES

Arizona Historical Society, Tucson, Arizona
"Reminiscences of Alvina Rosenda Contreras"
San Carlos Agency Records, M.S. 707, box 7 of 18, Letterbooks 39 and 210.

Arizona State Museum, Tucson, Arizona
"Reminiscences of Sherman Curley." Goodwin Papers, Folder 34.

National Archives Microfilm Publications, Washington, DC
Register of Enlistments, Indian Scouts, Volume 150 (1866–1874) and Volume
    153 (1882–1886) C680, C699, C722, C751, C772.

National Archives Trust
Carlisle Indian School Descriptive and Historical Record of Student. Apache
    Arizona Class of 1901. 5442 Alonzo Speeche.

University of Arizona Library, Tucson, Arizona
John Clum's Diary. Paper Drawer 1, Special Collections

NEWSPAPERS

Apache Scout (San Carlos, AZ)
Arizona Daily Citizen (Tucson, AZ)
Arizona Silver Belt (Globe, AZ)
Nevada State Journal (Reno, NV)
Prescott Courier (Prescott, AZ)
Weekly Arizonian (Tucson, AZ)

ONLINE SOURCES

Shadows at Dawn by Karl Jacoby with online references at www.brown.edu/aravaipa.

The 1887 Sonora Earthquake. A YouTube video by Phil Pearthree of the Arizona Geological Survey.

en.wikipedia.org/wiki/Valery_Havard.

ORAL INTERVIEWS

Lonnie Bullis, grandson of Capitan Chiquito. I lived with Lonnie from 1992 to 1999.

Delores Russel and Judy Nolan, granddaughters of Alonzo Bullis. Interview by author, 2003.

Mary O'Donnell interview by author. San Carlos, Arizona, June 2014.

Seth Pilsk, coordinator of the San Carlos Apache Elder's Council, interview by author on an herb walk in Aravaipa Canyon, April 2012.

Seth Pilsk interview by author, April 2014. San Carlos, Arizona. Seth was given this information from Hopi leaders visiting Fort Apache.

UNITED STATES FEDERAL REPORTS

Clum, John. 1875. Reports of Agents in Arizona, San Carlos. Annual Report of the Commissioner of Indian Affairs for the Year 1875. Washington, DC: Government Printing Office.

Colyer, Vincent. 1872. *Peace with the Apaches of New Mexico and Arizona: Report of Vincent Colyer, 1871.* Washington, DC: Government Printing Office.

Court of Claims. 1888. *Juan Elias vs. The United States and Apache Indians.* Indian Depredations. No. 7,550. www.brown.edu/Aravaipa.

Howard, O. O. 1872. *Letter of Brigadier General Howard to Major General Shofield from Camp McDowell, Arizona Territory, April 18, 1872.* Annual Report of the Department of the Interior, 1872. Washington, DC: Government Printing Office.

Kitch, James B. 1927. *Letter of James B. Kitch, Superintendent, United States Indian Field Service to the Commissioner of Indian Affairs,* Washington, DC, July 28, 1927. www.brown.edu/aravaipa.

Meritt, E. B. 1927. *Letter of E. B. Meritt, Assistant Commissioner, to the Secretary of the Interior, Office of Indian Affairs.* Washington, DC, July 18, 1927. www.brown.edu/aravaipa.

Terrell, John J. 1919. *Letter of John J. Terrell, Inspector in Charge, United States Indian Service, to the Commissioner of the General Land Office.* Washington, DC, June 24, 1919. www.brown.edu/aravaipa.

United States Census 1910.

BOOKS AND ARTICLES

Adams, David Wallace. 1995. *Education for Extinction.* Lawrence: University Press of Kansas.

Ball, Eve. 1980. *Indeh.* Norman: University of Oklahoma Press.

Barry, John M. 2009. *The Great Influenza: The Story of the Deadliest Pandemic in History*. London: Penguin Books.

Basso, Keith. 1979. *Portraits of the Whiteman: Linguistic Play and Cultural Symbols among the Western Apache*. Cambridge: Cambridge University Press.

Bolton, Herbert Eugene. 1936. *Rim of Christendom: A Biography of Eusebio Francisco Kino*. New York: Macmillan.

Bourke, John G. 1971. *On the Border with Crook*. Lincoln: University of Nebraska Press.

Burbank, E. A. 1944. *Burbank among the Indians*. Caldwell, ID: Caxton Printers.

Burns, Mike. 2010. *All of My People Were Killed: The Memoir of Mike Burns (Hoomothya), a Captive Indian*. Prescott, AZ: Sharlot Hall Museum.

Carmony, Neil B. 1997. *Apache Days and Tombstone Nights: John Clum's Autobiography, 1877–1887*. Silver City, NM: High-Lonesome Books.

Clark, LaVerne Harrell. 2001. *They Sang for Horses: The Impact of the Horse on Navajo and Apache Folklore*. Boulder: University Press of Colorado.

Clum, Woodworth. 1936. *Apache Agent: The Story of John P. Clum*. Cambridge, MA: Riverside Press.

Collins, Charles. 1999. *Apache Nightmare: The Battle at Cibecue Creek*. Norman: University of Oklahoma Press.

Colwell-Chanthaphonh, Chip. 2007. *Massacre at Camp Grant: Forgetting and Remembering Apache History*. Tucson: University of Arizona Press.

Colyer, Vincent. 1871. *Peace with the Apaches of New Mexico and Arizona*. Freeport, NY: Books for Libraries Press.

Cozzens, Peter. 2001. *The Struggle for Apacheria: Eyewitnesses to the Indian Wars, 1865–1890*. Mechanicsburg, PA: Stackpole Books.

Danielson, Helga. 1971. "Over-Kill in Apache Land." *Frontier Times*. June–July.

De La Garza, Phyllis. 1995. *The Apache Kid*. Tucson, AZ: Westernlore Press.

Dobyns, Henry F. 1981. *From Fire to Flood: Historic Human Destruction of Sonoran Desert Riverine Oases*. Socorro, NM: Ballena Press Anthropological Papers No. 20.

Forrest, Earle R., and Edwin B. Hill. 1947. *Lone War Trail of Apache Kid*. Pasadena, CA: Trail's End Publishing

Griffen, William B. 1988. *Apaches at War and Peace: The Janos Presidio, 1750–1858*. Norman: University of Oklahoma Press.

Goodwin, Grenville. 1969. *The Social Organization of the Western Apache*. Tucson: University of Arizona Press.

———. 1983. *Western Apache Raiding and Warfare*. Tucson: University of Arizona Press.

Hadley, Diana. 1991. *Environmental Changes in Aravaipa, 1870–1970: An Ethnoecological Survey*. Phoenix: Arizona State Office of the Bureau of Land Management. Cultural Resource Series, Monograph No. 7.

Haley, James L. 1997. *Apaches: A History and Culture Portrait*. Norman: University of Oklahoma Press.

Hayes, Jess G. 1954. *Apache Vengeance*. Albuquerque: University of New Mexico Press.

Howard, O. O., Major-General. 1907. *My Life and Experiences among Our Hostile Indians*. Hartford, CT: A. D. Worthington.

———.1908. *Famous Indian Chiefs I Have Known*. New York: Century.

Jackson, W. H. 1877. *Descriptive Catalogue of Photographs of North American Indians*. Washington, DC: Government Printing Office. Miscellaneous Publications No. 9.

Jacoby, Karl. 2008. *Shadows at Dawn: A Borderlands Massacre and the Violence of History*. New York: Penguin Press.

Kessell, John L. 1976. *Friars, Soldiers, and Reformers: Hispanic Arizona and the Sonora Mission Frontier, 1767–1856*. Tucson: University of Arizona Press.

Kielberg-McClenahan, P. J. 2013. *Journey to Aravaipa Canyon: Pioneers in the Territory of Arizona*. Bloomington, IN: iUniverse.

Lockwood, Frank C. 1987. *The Apache Indians*. Lincoln: University of Nebraska Press.

McCarty, Kieran. 1997. *A Frontier Documentary: Sonora and Tucson, 1821–1848*. Tucson: University of Arizona Press.

McKanna, Clare V., Jr. 2009. *Court-Martial of Apache Kid: The Renegade of Renegades*. Lubbock: Texas Tech University Press.

Meed, Douglas V. 1993. *They Never Surrendered: Bronco Apaches of the Sierra Madres, 1890–1935*. Tucson, AZ: Westernlore Press.

Moorhead, Max L. 1968. *The Apache Frontier: Jacobo Ugarte and Spanish-Indian Relations in Northern New Spain, 1769–1791*. Norman: University of Oklahoma Press.

Morris, John Miller, ed. 2002. *Narrative of the Coronado Expedition, By Pedro de Castaneda de Najera*. Chicago: Lakeside Press, R. R. Donnelley and Sons.

Nentvig, Juan, SJ. 1980. *Rudo Ensayo: A Description of Sonora and Arizona in 1764*. Translated, clarified and annotated by Alberto Francisco Pradeau and Robert R. Rasmussen. Tucson: University of Arizona Press.

Officer, James E. 1987. *Hispanic Arizona, 1536–1856*. Tucson: University of Arizona Press.

Ogle, Ralph Hedrick. 1970. *Federal Control of the Western Apaches, 1848–1886*. Albuquerque: University of New Mexico Press.

Olson, Donald W., and Laurie E. Jasinski. 2009. *Abraham Lincoln's Celestial Connections*. Cambridge, MA: Sky and Telescope.

Perry, Richard J. 1993. *Apache Reservation: Indigenous Peoples and the American State*. Austin: University of Texas Press.

Penfield, Thomas. 2004. *Dig Here!: Lost Mines and Buried Treasure of the Southwest*. Kempton, IL: Adventures Limited Press.

Radbourne, Allan. 2005. *Mickey Free: Apache Captive, Interpreter, and Indian Scout*. Tucson: Arizona Historical Society.

Randall, Kenneth A. 1995. *Only the Echoes: The Life of Howard Bass Cushing*. Las Cruces, NM: Yucca Tree Press.

Randall, Vincent, and Jeannette Cassa. 2002. *Western Apache Trees and Shrubs (Nigosdzan Bil Dagodotl'izhi)*. San Carlos, AZ: San Carlos Apache Tribe.

Record, Ian W. 2008. *Big Sycamore Stands Alone: The Western Apaches, Aravaipa, and the Struggle for Place*. Norman: University of Oklahoma Press.

Robinson, Charles M. 1949. *General Crook and the Western Frontier*. Norman: University of Oklahoma Press.

Robinson, Sherry. 2000. *Apache Voices: Their Stories of Survival as Told to Eve Ball*. Albuquerque: University of New Mexico Press.

Russell, Don. 2003. *One Hundred and Three Fights and Scrimmages: The Story of General Rueben F. Bernard*. Mechanicsburg, PA: Stackpole Books.

Santiago, Mark. 2011. *The Jar of Severed Hands: Spanish Deportation of Apache Prisoners of War, 1770–1810*. Norman: University of Oklahoma Press.

Schellie, Don. 1968. *Vast Domain of Blood: The Story of the Camp Grant Massacre*. Los Angeles: Westernlore Press.

Scott, Hugh Lenox. 1928. *Some Memories of a Soldier*. New York: Century.

Smith, Robert L. 1997. *Venomous Animals of Arizona*. Tucson: University of Arizona Press.

Stockel, H. Henrietta. 1993. *Survival of the Spirit: Chiricahua Apaches in Captivity*. Reno: University of Nevada Press.

———. 2004. *Shame and Endurance: The Untold Story of the Chiricahua Apache Prisoners of War*. Tucson: University of Arizona Press.

Sweeney, Edwin R. 1992. *Merejildo Grijalva: Apache Captive, Army Scout*. El Paso: Texas Western Press; University of Texas at El Paso.

Terrell, John Upton. 1972. *Apache Chronicle: The Story of the People*. New York: World Publishing; Times Mirror.

Thrapp, Dan L. 1967. *The Conquest of Apacheria*. Norman: University of Oklahoma Press.

Van Orden, Jay, and Mary Ellen Barnes. 2013. "When No One Had a Camera: An Artist-Participant Paints the Tully and Ochoa Wagon Train Fight." *Journal of Arizona History* 54, no. 3 (Autumn): 319–36.

Velasco, Jose F. 1865. *Continuación de la Estadística de Sonora*. Mexico City: Boletín de la Sociedad Mexicana de Geografia y Estadística.

Whitman, Royal E. 1871. *The Unpublished Personal Journal of Royal Emerson Whitman, First Lieutenant, US Army 3rd Cavalry*. Courtesy of his great-grandson Ross Blair.

Worcester, Donald E. 1979. *The Apaches: Eagles of the Southwest*. Norman: University of Oklahoma Press.

INDEX

Yeomen, Sharecroppers, and Socialists:
Plain Folk Protest in Texas, 1870–1914
Kyle G. Wilkison

More Zeal Than Discretion: The Westward
Adventures of Walter P. Lane
Jimmy L. Bryan

On the Move: A Black Family's Western Saga
S. R. Martin

Texas That Might Have Been: Sam Houston's
Foes Write to Albert Sidney Johnston
Margaret S. Henson

Tejano Leadership in Mexican and
Revolutionary Texas
Jesús F. De la Teja

Texas Left: The Radical Roots of
Lone Star Liberalism
David O. Cullen

How Did Davy Die? And Why Do We
Care So Much?
James E. Crisp and Dan Kilgore

Drumbeats from Mescalero: Conversa-
tions with Apache Elders, Warriors, and
Horseholders
H. Henrietta Stockel

Turmoil on the Rio Grande: History of the
Mesilla Valley, 1846–1865
William S. Kiser

Texas Right: The Radical Roots of
Lone Star Conservatism
David O' Donald Cullen and Kyle G.
Wilkison

We Never Retreat: Filibustering Expeditions
into Spanish Texas, 1812–1822
Ed Bradley

General Alonso de León's Expeditions into
Texas, 1686–1690
Lola Orellana Norris

Comanches and Germans on the Texas
Frontier: The Ethnology of Heinrich Berghaus
Daniel J. Gelo and Christopher J.
Wickham, with contributions by
Heide Castañeda

Murder and Intrigue on the Mexican Border:
Governor Colquitt, President Wilson,
and the Vergara Affair
John A. Adams

Woolly West: Colorado's Hidden History of
Sheepscapes
Andrew Gulliford

Preserving German Texan Identity: Reminis-
cences of William A. Trenckmann, 1859–1935
Walter L. Buenger

Civil War on the Rio Grande, 1846–1876
Roseann Bacha-Garza, Christopher L.
Miller, and Russell K. Skowronek

To the Vast and Beautiful Land: Anglo
Migration into Spanish Louisiana and
Texas, 1760s–1820s
Light Townsend Cummins

"Red Tom" Hickey: The Uncrowned
King of Texas Socialism
Peter Buckingham

The Great Texas Social Studies
Textbook War of 1961–1962
Allan O. Kownstar